SALT SPRING ISLAND
A Place To Be

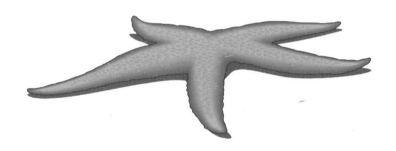

Ellie Thorburn & Pearl Gray

MARCH 1999

Heritage House

CANADIAN CATALOGUING IN PUBLICATION DATA

Thorburn, Ellie, 1947-
Salt Spring Island

ISBN 1-895811-27-9
1. Salt Spring Island (B.C.)
I. Gray, Pearl, 1948-
II. Title.
FC3845.S27T54 1997   971.1'28   C97-910137-9
F1089.S2T56 1997

First Edition 1998

Heritage House wishes to acknowledge Heritage Canada, the British Columbia Arts Council, the Ministry of Small Business, Tourism and Culture, and the Canada Council for supporting its publishing program.

Editor: Audrey McClellan
Cover design: Darlene Nickull
Book design: Catherine Mack, Cairn Consulting
Front cover photo: Ellie Thorburn (Sunrise on Fulford Harbour)
Back cover photos: Ellen Karpinski (top), Helen Tara (middle left and lower right), Ellie Thorburn (middle right), Anne Stevenson (lower left).

HERITAGE HOUSE PUBLISHING COMPANY LTD.
Unit #8 - 17921 55th Ave., Surrey, BC V3S 6C4

Printed in Canada

DEDICATION

To the memory of my parents
Ellie Thorburn

For my children, Samantha and Jason
Pearl Gray

ACKNOWLEDGEMENTS

THANK YOU TO THE MANY PEOPLE WE INTERVIEWED and all who gave so generously of their time. They included: Bob Akerman, who helped with his family history and provided photographs from the Akerman Museum; outdoorsman Jack Rosen, who contributed the piece on kayaking; bird-watcher Steve Coopman; our geologist mentor Jim Monger; Tony Richards of the *Gulf Islands Driftwood*, and Richard Mouat Toynbee, who were so generous with their photo archives; the Islands Trust Office, which provided documents and information; the many B&B operators who shared their specialty recipes and menus; author Charles Khan; Helen and Bob Tara, who loaned us photos and original out-of-print material; the Lions Club, which allowed us to use their fine map; Linda Adams, whose Recreation Map was a helpful reference; the countless artisans whose map we have reproduced; Anne Stevenson and Ellen Karpinski for scenic photos; Karey Litton and Marion Andrews, who supplied family photos; and Russ Crouse and his realtor colleagues who provided insight on the real estate scene. We wish to express our gratitude for the patience and candour of the many people interviewed and mentioned in conjunction with this book.

Finally we wish to thank our editor Audrey McClellan; Cathy Mack for her research, interviews, and insights; and our publisher Rodger Touchie. When the task grew larger than we ever thought possible, they were all there to support us.

Publisher's Prelude

OVER 140 YEARS, SALT SPRING ISLAND has evolved from an occasional native hunting ground to a year-round haven for residents and tourists alike. Salt Spring is a fitting choice to introduce the "A Place to Be" series on unique settings that offer a lifestyle, cultural dynamics, an admirable heritage, vibrant hospitality, and people truly worth celebrating.

The authors, Ellie Thorburn and Pearl Gray, share an enthusiasm for their ongoing discovery of things Salt Spring. Both have been islanders long enough to know "just about everything with a history and everybody with a reputation." Both agree that they will never take the natural beauty of Salt Spring for granted. They are island boosters to the core. As fate would have it, book designer Cathy Mack, a former employee of the *Gulf Islands Driftwood*, Salt Spring's popular newspaper, and now a resident of Vancouver Island, spent much of the 1980s and early '90s living on the island. "The stories I could tell..." Cathy says with a mischievous smile.

Much of Salt Spring's appeal and character comes from the distinct differences found within the community. It's that fragmented personality, its unusual governmental structure, even its geology of two parts that make it unique.

Here, Robert Bateman and hundreds of other artists, writers, poets, and artisans alike gain their creative inspiration in studios that dot the coves and valleys. Likewise, naturalists and dens of holistic healing abound. Folk singer Valdy is a local institution. Now urbanites descend on the Gulf Islands seeking a simpler life and an attractive climate.

The combination of new ideas, old traditions, and a heritage of multiracial harmony promises to yield an exciting future. With this in mind, *Salt Spring Island: A Place To Be* can only be regarded as a work in progress—hopefully one that will be accepted by the island population as representative of their being. Also may it serve as a means of insight to all who search for a place to BE.

Heritage House Publishing

CONTENTS

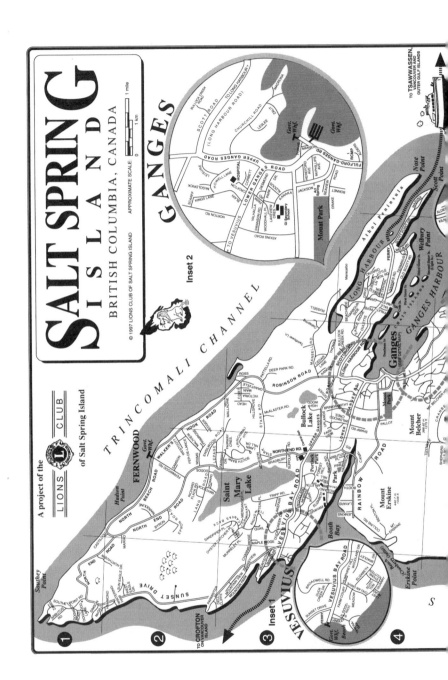

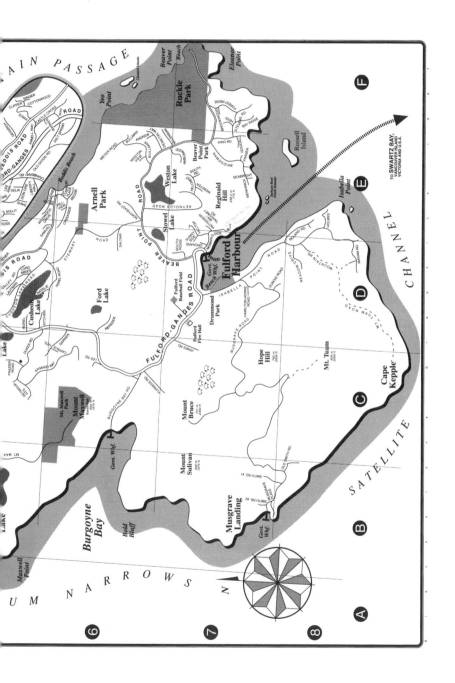

John Armstrong, buttermaker, stands in the doorway of Salt Spring Island Creamery (c. 1909). Erected in 1905, the creamery was owned by island farmers. When Arthur Drake was in charge, butter entered in major competitions won various prizes, including a Canada-wide trophy. The building now houses a bakery.

Jane Mouat and her sons bought Percy Purvis's store in 1905 and made it the focal point of Ganges commerce through most of the twentieth century. Brothers Gilbert, Gavin, and Will and their descendants have played a large role in the growth of the island. When winter storms isolated settlers around the coast, Gavin Mouat was known to fill his launch with supplies and make home deliveries.

Little Molly Akerman, seen on the Fulford-Ganges Road in 1905. The family home and Mount Maxwell are in the background.

1

SETTLING

In Unsettling Times

A CURIOUS CONDITION EXISTED in the colonies of Vancouver Island and British Columbia in 1859, and that condition posed a dilemma for the colonial governor of the day, James Douglas. He had set an honourable precedent by allowing legal settlement only on land which he had bought from the local First Nations peoples through treaty negotiations and had surveyed. In other words, Douglas seemed reluctant to resell what he didn't legally own.

His problem was that in 1859, Forty-Niners from California were flowing into Victoria at an alarming rate while other gold seekers were returning to the B.C. coast from the Fraser River, intent on settling there to either lick their wounds or enjoy their newfound wealth. Douglas rarely had extra cash lying about, and Hudson's Bay Company head office in London was unwilling to supply more for further treaties, so he was never in possession of excess surveyed land. When there was a sudden rise in demand for acreage, he had a problem.

That short-term problem was solved—and a long-term one created—by a clever Scot named John Copland. Copland not only resolved the land shortage problem, but he also devised a scheme that would allow him and his mates to pay for their plots. A lawyer by profession, Copland was a former resident of Australia who arrived on the governor's doorstep most willing to explain the concept of pre-emption. In simple terms, this strategy allowed settlers to claim a chunk of land and work it as they saw fit until the government had the time and inclination to survey it. Only then would they have to pay, and with any luck they would be in a position, through their hard work, to do so. Of course the one group ignored in Copland's scheme was the Hul'qumi'num (Salish) people, a loose collection of First Nations that traditionally inhabited many areas along the coast on a seasonal basis. Probably because they were more preoccupied by their northern enemies, the Haida and Heiltsuk, the Cowichan and other southern tribes watched peacefully as the new settlers encroached upon the land. In the short term the new faces were accepted. In the long term, pre-emption would come to be portrayed as an illegal land grab.

In July 1859, John Copland and 29 other settlers were authorized to stake their claims to 100 acres per man or 200 per family on Tuam Island. Tuam Island was a seasonal home for the Cowichan people, where they collected clams and berries and other bounties, but little heed was given to that detail and a mixture of Europeans, Polynesians, transplanted American blacks, a few Portuguese, and a few Anglos soon headed up the Saanich Peninsula toward their new home.

Today the name Tuam is reserved only for the dominant mountain at the south end of the island. The island itself is known far and wide as Saltspring.

ISLAND OF MANY NAMES

Given the brief extent of its history, the largest of B.C.'s Gulf Islands has worn many monikers. The Cowichan people called it Chu-an, *meaning "facing the sea." This was anglicized to* Tuan. *When a few Irish settlers got a hold of it they modified the spelling to* Tuam *in honour of the Galway town so-called.*

James Douglas referred to Chuan, *in 1853 correspondence to his Hudson's Bay Company superiors, as an island where "many salt springs exist." While early settlers took this simple description as a name for their newfound home, the official surveyor, Captain George Henry Richards, would have none of it. In retrospect, Richards seemed hellbent on naming everything on the island after some aspect of his navy, while locals were resolute in calling their home* Salt Spring. *The name* Admiral Island *became a fixture on government maps until 1906, when officialdom surrendered to the will of the people. It should be noted that this capitulation did nothing but encourage the islanders, and bureaucracy has found them a stubborn bunch ever since. In a sinister act of subversion, the spelling* Saltspring *has gradually come to dominate government literature. They simply can't leave well enough alone!*

The choice of the people shall be the choice of the editors. Henceforth we use Salt Spring *wherever possible.*

THE EARLY SETTLERS

From its earliest settlement, Salt Spring Island can boast a heritage of multiculturalism and racial tolerance. Men and women of various races have played roles developing this timeless place. While the first formal settlement on the island was organized by a Scottish lawyer, only a few of the early settlers were from Great Britain. It was blacks from California, Hawaiians, and a cluster of young Australians who chose Salt Spring as their new home.

The earliest boatloads of settlers would land at Ganges Harbour and Vesuvius Bay, favouring the northern end of the island to settle. As a result, two makeshift communities started to take shape in this area in the early years. Central Settlement was fittingly named (still called Central, it is today the intersection of four roads south of St. Mary Lake) and the site of the island's first school. A second settlement, near today's Fernwood on the northeast coast, was anchored by settler Johnathan Begg's general store and nursery. The first commercial business was a sandstone quarry started at Vesuvius in 1860.

In the south, Kanakas and a few Anglo farmers selected more remote settings to build a new life.

Willis Stark was a marksman. Cougars frequently swam across from Vancouver Island and caused havoc among the flocks of sheep. According to the journals of Reverend E.F. Wilson, Willis was one of 40 "coloured or partly coloured people" still living on Salt Spring in 1895.

Salt Spring's First Schoolteacher

Much myth surrounds early Salt Spring's "black colony," which was not a colony at all. Because many settlers abandoned their pre-empted land after harsh winters in the early 1860s, leaving the hardy black homesteaders as a majority, some newsmen deemed it a colony. While all this was going on, one intelligent black man with a degree from an Ohio college and a recognized teaching certificate set out to do some educating close to home. One of the original 29 authorized to claim land on Salt Spring, John C. Jones opened the first school on the island he had rapidly come to love. In 1861, at Jones' urging and to the delight of Reverend Ebenezer Robson, all settlers banded together to build a log structure in Central Settlement at the crossroads north of Ganges. The cabin was to serve as both school and church.

For several years, with endless gratitude but no pay, John C. Jones acted as the Salt Spring teacher. Finally in 1869, after island residents once more pointed to their eighteen school-age children and their reliance on his good will, government officials agreed to officially hire him for $500 per year.

Say,
Without any pay
For ten years to teach school
One must be drunk or a fool!
John C. Jones was neither.
He was a teacher!

The Harbour House Hotel in Ganges was operated from 1902 to 1964 by the Crofton family. When the original proprietor, Fred Crofton, went to war in 1916, his wife Nora (a daughter of Reverend E.F. Wilson) ran the hotel. Among the historic murals that embellished the interior of the pub was one of John C. Jones.

John Whims (left) and Willis Stark were the sons of two of Salt Spring's earliest black settlers. After the Civil War, many American blacks returned south. The Whims and Stark families stayed into the twentieth century.

The Blacks on Salt Spring

The first Salt Spring settlers faced a harsh winter in 1859-60, and many Anglos left in search of less challenging pastures. Cherishing the true freedom they had found, the black community struggled onward. As a result of this determination, a majority of the 21 homesteads located north of Ganges Harbour in 1861 were occupied by black families that had escaped repression further south. Men who pre-empted land included Armstead Buckner, Abraham Copeland, William Robinson, John Craven Jones, William Isaacs, and Hiram Whims.

The diaries of Reverend Ebenezer Robson, who spread the gospel among the early island communities, speak highly of the hard-working black settlers. One family he was partial to were the Starks, who arrived in 1860. In the company of a white trader named McCauley, Lewis Stark, his pregnant wife Sylvia, four-year-old son Willis, baby Emma, and their herd of fifteen

Sitting on his plough enjoying his pipe in 1941, John Whims worked the same fields father Hiram had cleared 90 years earlier.

cows came ashore in Vesuvius Bay with the aid of a young Cowichan couple.

The Starks settled in a remote log cabin and proved successful in building their herd and crop farming. In the late 1860s, tragedy struck twice when two farm hands, William Robinson and Giles Curtis, were murdered in successive years.

The Starks relocated closer to Ganges on a farm they called Fruitvale, but the killings haunted the family and Lewis decided to pre-empt land near Nanaimo. After two years he moved his family there in 1875, leaving his Salt Spring property in the hands of nineteen-year-old Willis. Twenty-one years later, Lewis himself was found dead at the bottom of a cliff. He was 85 and it was alleged by the Stark family that a henchman of coal baron James Dunsmuir had done the deed.

Sylvia Stark returned to Salt Spring to live with her son Willis at Fruitvale and was known far and wide as Aunt Silvey. She died in 1944 at age 106.

The Kanakas of Salt Spring

An equally fascinating role in the settlement of the Gulf Islands was played by the people who called themselves Kanakas, which translates from their native Polynesian to mean "human beings." There were Kanakas on the west coast of Vancouver Island as early as the 1780s, when fur traders descended on Nootka Sound in quest of sea otter pelts. As the Hudson's Bay Company expanded its presence in the early nineteenth century, Kanakas made up anywhere from a quarter to half the work force that built and maintained its forts. Governor James Douglas held the Kanakas in high esteem and relied on them heavily both at Fort Victoria and in one of British Columbia's most peculiar controversies.

As early as 1850, Douglas had recruited sixteen Kanakas to build

---

ISABELLA POINT OR KANAKA POINT?

In his very readable account of early island life, Salt Spring Sagas, *Eric Roberts refers to the legend of Kanaka ship jumpers in the 1860s who apparently had an affinity for Isabella Point. The captain of the SS* Parisian, *a Pacific trading ship, tried passing Salt Spring after repeatedly losing Kanaka crew. According to Roberts, "The recurrent losses annoyed the skipper who threatened to have every Kanaka placed in irons while passing Salt Spring."*

Peavine Kahou's old log cabin, said to be haunted, still stands in Ruckle Park. After his wife Mary died with her twins while giving birth, Kahou left the island.

On May 10, 1880, a congregation of Kanakas, Indians, and European settlers attended the consecration of St. Paul's Catholic Church. Land for the church was donated by Horace Shepherd, a settler whose two sons, Bill and George, married Kanaka women. George married Julia Naukana, daughter of William (right).

The windows, door, altar, and lumber were brought from the Stone Church at Cowichan Bay by natives in three canoes lashed together. Ted Akerman used a "stoneboat" and oxen to transport the load from Burgoyne Bay to Fulford where it stands today.

KANAKA QUEEN

Maria Mahoy, left
at 30, above with
daughter Mary
Jane (Fisher)
Roberts, and right at
80. Mary Jane raised
her family on Salt Spring
and is buried with her mother
near St. Paul's Church.

Maria Mahoy first came to Salt Spring Island as a teenage mother
and wife of whaling captain Abel Douglas in 1871. By the mid-1880s,
with a brood of six and an oft-absent husband, Maria had befriended
neighbour William Haunea and in his later years she cared for him.

About the same time, either abandoned or frustrated by her
husband's long absence, Maria started a relationship with nearby
farmer George Fisher, son of an English settler and Cowichan mother.
George and Maria had another six children in a relationship that
lasted over 50 years.

On his death, Haunea bequeathed Russell Island, at the mouth
of Fulford Harbour, to Maria. There she and George built a successful
farm including fruit orchards and a small sheep flock. Harvesting
both their crops and the island shoreline for clams, crab, herring roe,
and octopus, this family of fourteen led a rustic life without
refrigeration or electricity. Daily, George or Maria would row the
children across to Beaver Point so they could attend school.

After her family grew and dispersed, Maria and George
remained on Russell Island, hosting festive gatherings for their
friends and neighbours. Beloved by all, Maria died an octogenarian in
1936. Her children, grandchildren, and great-grandchildren now live
throughout B.C.

and settle his fort at Victoria. As their regiment grew and their reliability and accommodating ways reinforced his impressions, Douglas faced a new problem. The ever-acquisitive Americans were laying claim to Douglas' San Juan Islands, east of Fort Victoria in the Strait of Georgia. Douglas rectified the problem by sending foreman Charles Griffin and a contingent of Kanaka settlers to the San Juans with an army of over a thousand sheep. Possession was known to be a substantial portion of the law, but a few American settlers made similar claims. Over the next score of years a series of confrontations and follies unfolded. History would call them the Pig War.

KANAKA: THE UNTOLD STORY

In 1995, Salt Spring resident Tom Koppel's detailed tribute to the Kanaka settlers was published. This book, **Kanaka: The Untold Story of Hawaiian Pioneers in British Columbia and the Pacific Northwest,** *is a fascinating story that has been used to prepare this summary.*

The Kanakas of San Juan Island, long associated with their own Hawaiian monarchy, were more at ease with the British form of government than the American republic. As a result, when a European arbitrator deemed the San Juan Islands to be a U.S. possession, most of the Kanakas, led by William Naukana moved their families across Haro Strait to the Gulf Islands. In the mid-1870s, while Naukana and his partner and son-in-law John Palua settled nearby Portland Island (current home of tranquil Princess Margaret Marine Park), a number of Kanakas pre-empted land bordering on Salt Spring's Fulford Harbour. Kanaka households ranged from Isabella Point to parts of what is now Ruckle Park, where Peavine Kahou's old log cabin still stands.

Many of these Hawaiian settlers had been introduced to the Roman Catholic faith by missionaries in their homeland, and they were major contributors to the construction of St. Paul's, the quaint Fulford Harbour church that has long been a favourite subject of photographers and artists. After a school was built at Beaver Point, William Naukana moved his large family to Salt Spring to aid their education. Between one and two dozen households headed by Hawaiians were prominent in the southern Gulf Islands until the turn of the century. While it was quite precise with the origins of other settlers, the unofficial 1895 census by Reverend E.F. Wilson lumped the Kanakas in with "half breeds" and "partly coloured." Only six were acknowledged as "Sandwich Islanders."

With time and new generations of mixed marriages, the Kanaka profile melded into the heritage of Salt Spring. In August 1994, about 300 Kanaka descendants from B.C. and Washington state gathered for a reunion and luau on the shores of Fulford Harbour. Fittingly, a bronze plaque, since mounted at St. Paul's Catholic Church, was unveiled by Don Watt and Tony Farr of the Salt Spring Island Historical Society.

Aussies Galore! —and a Few Portuguese

Australia itself had only been settled since 1787, when eleven British ships containing 537 male and 180 female convicts landed in today's Sydney Harbour. A penal colony first and a commercial settlement more by accident than choice, Australia soon bred a second generation of settlers, many of whom were raised clearing farmland and practised in the art of agriculture. Others were trained as miners. A substantial contingent returned to northern climes, lured primarily by the exaggerated rumours of California gold. With that woeful adventure behind them, a band of impoverished, disillusioned Aussies scraped together the $35 fare to get from San Francisco to Victoria in the late 1850s. They were back on British soil and fortunately they were in the company of John Copland.

Copland was a stubborn Edinburgh lawyer who had spent six years in Australia and had come to Victoria via San Francisco. In short order he saw that Governor James Douglas had done little to promote settlement beyond the immediate needs of the Hudson's Bay Company. Gaining Douglas' ear, he pointed out that the vast influx of Yankee gold seekers spelled potential doom for British jurisdiction. Eventually the arguments of his Committee for Settlement of Salt Spring Island were heard and his settlement proposal accepted.

While Copland's main audience was Aussies, documents show that the first 25 approved settlers included Scots, Irish, English and American black ex-slaves as well. The first ship of seventeen settlers left Victoria for the north end of Salt

Spring on July 27, 1859. By year's end a total of 70 farmers, including 53 Aussies, were preparing to face their first winter. There were also two sets of Portuguese brothers, the Bittancourts near Vesuvius and the Nortons near St. Mary Lake, who pre-empted land. For years the Bittancourts' schooner provided islanders with a lifeline to Victoria as ship passage was sporadic at best.

Although Copland's settlement effort was backed by many, he received little support from the Victoria establishment. The fact that he was inexplicably ruled the loser of Salt Spring's first election to the colonial legislature suggests skullduggery in high places. In spite of his admirable accomplishment in leading the settlement of the island, Copland has been given only limited acknowledgement by B.C. historians. Eventually, after practising law in Victoria, he returned to Scotland with his wife.

A WAR OF POLITICS

The ensuing three decades of settlement on Salt Spring were patchy at best. During the 1860s, many would-be farmers worked at clearing the land only to be devastated by harsh winters, disease, or Indian attack. Others opted for opportunities elsewhere, in the gold fields of the Interior or the streets of Victoria. A few yearned for their homelands. By the mid-1860s fewer than 50 families remained, mostly growing food crops, cattle, and sheep. Later in the decade, fruit orchards yielded good crops which farmers were able to sell readily in Victoria and New Westminster.

Independent by nature, settlers on different parts of the island found themselves at odds in 1872. It is ironical that Salt Spring's greatest community schism was self-imposed. The rift came during a period of relative calm when a small group of citizens lobbied Victoria to incorporate the island as a township. Over the next decade, neighbours who had faced the worst of times together turned hostile. A small group of elected officials stubbornly ignored the protests of their neighbours. The debate raged hot and the rhetoric was full of venom. In the end we choose to remember the eloquent words of pioneer Theodore Trege as he celebrated the 1883 annulment of documents that had established local government. The words apply as much today as then:

We have had the experience of what happens when a small section of the people elevate themselves at the expense of the majority, without regard to the will of the ordinary people. We hope our children, our children's children and all who follow, will remember our experience and remain vigilant in the defence of what we so hardly secured on this island [Salt Spring], the right to live our lives as we see fit, in peace, in dignity and without interference.

At least one historic account notes that in 1884, when Beaver Point pioneer Henry Ruckle convinced Samuel and Emily Beddis to settle their family on southern Salt Spring, there were only twelve white families resident on the entire island. The fate of Beddis was one that all too often befell the hard-working newcomer. While Samuel managed to plant a substantial orchard, carve a trail north to Ganges Harbour, and, with the help of his sons, build a one-room school, his industry was ill-rewarded. During the extreme winter of 1893 he caught pneumonia. Emily and two of her sons rowed all night to carry Samuel to a Victoria hospital, but he died there at age 43.

One tragedy that probably had more effect on island settlement than it has been credited with was the smallpox epidemic of the mid-1860s. The broad sweep of death in native villages along the coast caused chaos in the natives' social hierarchy and left an air of suspicion and resentment toward the Europeans who had brought disease to the coast. While the relationship between individual settlers (many took Indian wives) and the nearby native villages was mainly friendly, a few renegade warriors wreaked havoc. One white settler protested to the *Colonist* newspaper in Victoria that there were more white casualties of Indian assault in the Gulf Islands than in the rest of B.C. combined.

In 1885, Thomas Mouat arrived to acquire 153 acres beside St. Mary Lake. Mouat also bought the home of original black settler Abraham Copeland, who was moving to Victoria.

In the same year, the island's first jail was built but only confined five occupants over the next decade. Two brawlers, one rustler, and two game poachers were the culprits. With the exception of a few Indian tribal clashes in the sur-

Henry and Ann Stevens (left) ran the north island's main boarding house at Central after 1887. Nephew Walter (seated right) later ran the house and farm. Joel Broadwell (right) and his wife had the largest farm on the island at the time, on today's Broadwell Mountain.

Over the years the CPR's coastal fleet connected islanders to the mainland. The Island Princess, Motor Princess, and Princess Patricia (seen here at Ganges) served the route from the 1920s until BC Ferries was formed in the 1950s.

In 1894, children from the surrounding farms were transported to and from the Central Settlement log school building on Ed Hamson's ox-drawn cart.

In 1930, Sam Matson of Vancouver Island Coach bought the old Island Princess from CPR and refitted it as the MV Cy Peck to carry Salt Spring Islanders to Swartz Bay. The ferry started a long career on September 27, 1930.

John P. Booth was a respected settler and the island's main politician in the nineteenth century. His funeral was the most well attended in the island's pioneer history.

rounding waters and the odd confrontation with non-resident thieves, Salt Spring had become a fairly tame place.

By 1894 only two of the original 1859 shipload of settlers remained on their pre-empted lands, John P. Booth and former HBC factor Henry Sampson. Of the first black settlers, only the Stark and Whims children still farmed their parents' land. Many, like teacher John C. Jones, returned to their place of birth. Others less fortunate, like William Robinson, had been killed.

Many families who had arrived in the early 1860s were still prominent as a new century neared. The Akermans, Maxwells, Nortons, Fred Foord and Ted Trege—all were active in their enterprise.

AN EARLY BIOGRAPHER

One of the most fascinating accounts of nineteenth-century life on the B.C. coast is by Reverend Edward F. Wilson, who came to Salt Spring with wife Fanny and ten children in 1894. Wilson was an imposing man, powerful in both stature and personality. He had spent over 25 years working in Indian communities as he slowly moved west from Ontario after emigrating from England in 1868 as an Anglican missionary. After a short stay on Vancouver Island, Victoria's Bishop Perrin offered Wilson the Salt Spring parish.

The reverend bought a 100-acre farm near Central Settlement that had first been cultivated by one of the original black settlers, Armstead Buckner. He moved into Stevens' boarding house to oversee construction of a substantial addition to Buckner's original cabin that would house his large family. Named Barnsbury, the farmhouse would eventually be the home of son Norman Wilson, who in 1930 built the island's acclaimed nine-hole golf course. At one stage the house functioned as a clubhouse, but it succumbed to flames in the mid-1960s.

A man of many talents, Wilson wrote his observations

REVEREND EDWARD FRANCIS WILSON

Excerpts from Reverend E.F. Wilson's Salt Spring Island, British Columbia, 1895 *include:*

As clearing land is expensive, there is a vast difference between the price of cleared land under cultivation, and that which is still primeval forest. The market value of the former is from $50.00 to $125 per acre...while the latter may be purchased from $7.00 to $15.00 per acre...The chief wants felt by the settlers were a doctor...a family hotel...a good general store...a shoe maker...telegraphic communication with Vancouver Island...more frequent steamboat service...more settlers.

During the winter and early spring...bays and inlets are alive with water fowl of all descriptions...Salt Spring Island is certainly an El Dorado for the sportsman.

The most ubiquitous and the most mischievous of the winged tribe are the blue jay and the American robin.

One man relates how he and his father shot nine panthers between them within a few weeks one autumn.

Here in the islands on the Pacific coast the climate is mild...no dread of an intense cold winter, no fear of drought in summer...no lack of fuel...crops can be gathered in almost invariably in good condition.

The farmer's wives all say...more is made by selling the eggs than by raising young birds.

on his new home shortly after coming to the island, using a $100 grant from the provincial government to finance his entertaining historical overview.

A magnetic if austere individual, Edward Wilson won wide respect for his dedication. He raised money to finish building St. Mary's Church near Fulford, and most Sundays thereafter he preached to congregations at both ends of the island. Over fifteen years he baptized, wedded, and buried the Anglicans of Salt Spring. At five weddings, his sought-after daughters Evelyn, Winnie, Kathleen, Flossie, and Nora were the brides. In 1904 he presided at the funeral of original settler John P. Booth. Reverend Wilson retired for a short period to California and died in Victoria in 1915.

When Reverend Wilson first came to Salt Spring he bought the dilapidated former home of Armstead Buckner, the only black among the first seventeen settlers authorized to pre-empt land in 1859.

Reverend Wilson had his Victoria home dismantled in 1894 and rebuilt on Salt Spring, adding to what he called "a rickety old log house [where] cattle and sheep had evidently been in and out at will."

After 1930 it became the golf course clubhouse. It later was lost to fire.

Reverend Wilson left his five sons ten-acre plots, and his five daughters all married local men. Many descendants survive on Salt Spring today.

THE AKERMANS—A LEGACY OF PIONEERING

Less than 150 years ago, when the first settlers came to a remote, primitive land that was managed by the Hudson's Bay Company, the survival rate was anything but encouraging. Harsh winters, heavy forests, disease, and the lure of Cariboo gold all worked against the dedicated homesteader. Yet in different pockets around British Columbia, a few unique families of stubborn, industrious men and women started a legacy that would see their offspring bonded to the same land five and six generations later.

In the Akerman family, long-time residents of the Fulford Valley, Salt Spring Island boasts an outstanding example of West Coast pioneers. Over six generations, one family has demonstrated both commitment to a chosen home and an unswerving focus on the land.

Joe and Martha Akerman (left) sit in front of Traveller's Rest with family and friends.

Traveller's Rest still stands on the Akerman property today, covered in ivy and visible from Fulford-Ganges Road. In recent years its main occupants have been children playing "haunted house."

Joseph Akerman, a transplanted English market gardener born in Wiltshire in 1838, arrived in Victoria on the *Tynemouth* at age seventeen. He held a job as a longshoreman in New Westminster and at one time is said to have cultivated a vegetable plot on the future site of Victoria's legislative buildings. In 1860 Joseph used his savings to settle in the Burgoyne (later called Fulford) Valley. The first year he built a log cabin in the shadows of Mount Bruce on the northwest side of the valley road, but after a cold winter in the mountain shadows he started a second home in a sunnier location—where the grand, derelict Traveller's Rest still stands today.

Joseph Akerman was in Victoria when Martha Clay and her two sisters disembarked the bride ship *Robert Lowe* in early 1863. After a wedding on May 14, 1863, Martha joined her new husband, Joseph, and became the second white woman resident of Salt Spring. On their farm the couple raised eight children and ran the island's first hotel, the Traveller's Rest. In concert with fellow settlers John Maxwell and Mike Gyves, Joe spent 37 years clearing and cultivating the land of the Burgoyne/Fulford area.

As the 1920s roared elsewhere, this bevy of Fulford Harbour beauties went swimming. Bob Akerman identifies his three sisters among the group. (L to R) Deena Cotsford, Molly Akerman, Eliza Maxwell, Dorothy Akerman, Inez Maxwell, and Tilly Akerman.

The Akerman clan

Valley schoolteacher A.W. Cooke, Joseph Akerman, and Mike Gyves stand behind Martha Akerman, Joe Jr., and Fanny and her husband Joe Nightingale, 1890s.

Martha was one of 36 young women aboard the Robert Lowe. *She was soon swept away to become the first white woman on south Salt Spring.*

Ted (left), Joseph, and three more of his sons harvest hay. In the background is the original home (still standing but much enlarged) that Ted built when he married Mike and Tuwa Gyves' daughter, Ellen.

Ted built his home beside the main road in 1897 and in 1916, with five children, he completed a two-storey addition. Ted and Ellen were widely respected throughout the island community.

Edward (Ted) Akerman and Ellen had five children who in turn gave them twenty grandchildren. Eleven of these were son Bob's brood, and he and wife Molly alone had 30 grandchildren and 21 great-grandchildren. Ted and Ellen have over 125 direct descendants born in this century and we are still counting!

During World War Two, third-generation Akerman, Bob, started raising sheep to support his family. Here in 1957 he has two young helpers Danny and Patrick.

Early in his days on Salt Spring, the Akerman's neighbour Mike Gyves had befriended the Cowichan people who often visited Burgoyne Bay to gather clams. There he met an attractive woman who would become his wife— Tuwa'h'wiye' George, daughter of a Cowichan hereditary chief. Tuwa was the first midwife on southern Salt Spring and brought many pioneer children, a number of them Akermans, into the world. Tuwa's own first daughter, Ellen Gyves, was born in 1871.

Meanwhile, Joseph and Martha Akerman were running a bustling household that would eventually include three daughters and five sons. Martha is reputed to have saved her eldest daughter, Fanny, from a cougar she found sniffing in her outdoor crib one day while she did her chores. On another occasion, when the growl of a prowling cat distracted Martha as she prepared dinner, Joseph took charge. With a plate of hot food uppermost in his mind he said to his wife, "Look thee to thy pots and pans, Martha, and I'll look to my panthers." He shot the intruder and came back in for his meal. Martha Akerman lived well into her nineties and instilled in the Akermans the genes of longevity that still reign today.

In 1895 the 355-acre family farm raised cattle, sheep, and poultry and boasted a productive 300-tree fruit orchard. After 35 years in the valley, Joe told chronicler Reverend E.F. Wilson that a homesteader "could not strike an easier place to live in. Crops are always sure. I have never known the fruit crop to fail," he said. "Two years out of three the trees are overloaded and break the branches down."

In time Joe and Martha's sons became farmers. In the new century, with growing competition from Okanagan and Fraser Valley farmers, being a Salt Spring farmer meant doing something else just to survive. Third son George Edward (Ted) built many of the island's early roads and was a justice of the peace for 45 years. He was a long-time secretary of the school board and often took on the practical rural role of "fence viewer" or surveyor to settle any boundary disputes.

In 1898 Ted married Ellen Gyves, Mike and Tuwa's daughter, and between 1902 and 1912 they in turn had five children—Molly, Dorothy, Tilly, Jim, and Bob. By 1928, young Jim was working at the valley's creamery. While the

Depression set in elsewhere, Jim took on a Ford truck and the cream route that ran from the Ruckle farm (near today's provincial park) across the Fulford Valley to the shadows of Mount Maxwell. The girls all married but stayed close at hand to raise their families. Young Bob remained on the farm and gradually took more responsibility for the homestead. Eventually Bob's older brother, Jim, left the island to raise his family in Quesnel.

The Cowichan heritage of his mother would have a lasting impact on Bob. Throughout his adult life, Bob has collected artifacts and craft pieces from native village life. In the early 1990s, Bob and Jim, both in their 80s, built a log museum beside Bob and Molly's home to display this collection. Perched next to the Fulford-Ganges Road, little more than a stone's throw from the original Traveller's Rest hotel building, the private museum is open to the public whenever Bob is home.

Like his grandfather Joseph and father Ted, Bob Akerman chose an amazing woman to marry. She held a special place in the hearts of many, as through the years she became the matriarch of the Fulford Valley. Molly (Morrison) Akerman, mother of eleven and an avid softball player well into her 70s, died in the spring of 1998. At the time of her death, she and Bob had 30 grandchildren and 21 great-grandchildren. Five sons and one daughter still reside near the original homestead. Many of their descendants live on their own properties on Salt Spring Island. Until two years before her passing, Molly commonly served Christmas dinner to a family gathering of 50.

Bob and Molly Akerman on the occasion of their 50th wedding anniversary on July 1, 1989. The celebration on the family acreage overlooking Fulford Harbour was attended by more than 80 family and friends.

THE TWENTIETH CENTURY

Sheep and dairy farming plus an assortment of orchards remained the island's main source of income in the Edwardian decade. The populations of both Vancouver and Victoria continued to expand and local foodstuffs were in demand.

Steamships arrived at Salt Spring a couple of times a week, and a small launch called *The Elf* took passengers from Fulford to Sidney every day. There, with the advent of the auto, you could board a Flying Line touring car to continue into Victoria.

After World War I the island became a hardball haven as teams from Fulford and Ganges travelled by fishboat to play Sidney and Victoria rivals.

With the onset of the Depression, players could no longer afford ball gloves, so they switched to softball. Bob Akerman, on behalf of the island's athletic commission, went to Victoria to get a bat, a ball, and catcher and first base gloves. Softball has been the game of choice ever since. It held more appeal for the women of the 1930s, who made the game a focal point of Saturday social life at Fulford Hall throughout the summer.

In 1940, with war at hand, the Akerman's built a diamond on their property to give local kids a place to play. This field, still in use, is now maintained by Parks and Recreation.

The Akermans had enough kids for their own team, and many of the grandchildren have carried on the tradition. Molly pitched until she was 75 and now Salt Spring's most valuable player award in women's softball is called the Molly Akerman trophy.

Basketball was another popular sport. Three teams of players (two men's and one women's) would cross the waters from Vancouver Island to Salt Spring to play the locals. Most often they brought an orchestra!

After the games, everyone made their way to Fulford Hall for a dance that lasted well into the night before an armada of small boats headed home to Sidney.

Bob Akerman bought his first car, a 1914 Model T, in 1928 when he was fifteen. It helped him get up to Ganges and the Harbour House dances where he met Molly.

This 1890s sawmill helped process wood as more farmland was cleared.

Harry Bullock's 300-acre farm, seen here in 1911, sat beside today's Bullock Lake and thrived for many years. Harry was widely known as "the Squire," and his home was the centre of social life at the turn of the century.

For 140 years, sheep have been the dominant animals in Salt Spring farming.

During the Depression, Bob recalls falling timber all day with a crosscut saw for two dollars. "Money was scarce and often workers were paid with product or farm produce," he recalls. In 1938 while working at a sawmill, Bob was paid with the lumber he used to start a home for his bride-to-be.

AFTER THE WAR

In the post-war era, Salt Spring faced the same upheaval as many rural Canadian communities. Prosperity in the cities, good jobs with attractive pay cheques, and restless youth led to a gradual emigration away from people's roots. Many of the orchard farms were let go and retirees became the main beachcombers. Then came the "hippie invasion" and another layer of humanity was added to the cake.

By this time many old-timers, like author Bea Hamilton, had seen a host of transients come and go. She recognized that a new generation would shape the future. In her enjoyable *Salt Spring Island*, published in 1969, Bea saw tides of change on her waterfront. Change and resistance to change would be the only constants. "For so it has always been," she wrote. To the newcomers she concluded:

> *I hope from time to time they'll give a thought to the staunch little band of pioneers who, first tasting the milk and honey of this favored isle, persevered through hardship to establish homes and families. They provide the drama of our history and we are proud of them.*

In 1949 the 160-foot Motor Princess *could carry 40 cars and 250 passengers from Fulford to Swartz Bay on Vancouver Island in half an hour. By then the MV* Cy Peck *was an inter-island vessel. Some say, "Give us the good old days!"*

2

THE GEOLOGY
& The Geography

HOW DO YOU EXPLAIN **750 MILLION YEARS** of geological history
to a generation raised on 30-second sound bites? That is the
dilemma that has faced Salt Spring resident Jim Monger
through his professional career. A geology professor at Simon
Fraser University in Vancouver, Jim and his wife, Jackie,
live in Vesuvius. As you will see, that means he is not a
Wrangellian.

Explaining the geological makeup of Salt Spring is no
small task, but Jim provided a capsule report to help put it
in perspective. First he explained that most of B.C.'s best
oceanfront property lay east of Revelstoke for about 570
million years. "West of this was a vast ocean, the ancestor of
the Pacific," Jim related, "across which were scattered chains
of volcanic islands like present-day Japan or the Aleutian
Islands."

Geology is a discipline largely based on scientific theory
about rock forms and their structure. Ultimately, different
types of rock created millions of years apart can end up next
to each other on some land mass like Salt Spring. By studying
faults, folds, sediment accumulation, volcanism, erosion,
mountain making, glaciation, and "the grain of the green,"
geologists can explain the oddities of any rock formation. In
the scheme of things, Salt Spring is quite odd. It might be
best described with a word applied to many of its residents—
non-conforming.

Before diving into pre-history, let us explain "grain of
the green." Any aerial photo that shows the Gulf Islands
and Vancouver Island gives the immediate impression that
all land masses set up from southeast to northwest. It's as if
some giant rake had been pulled repeatedly in this direction,
creating coves, fjords, and bays like Fulford Harbour. This
dominant geological grain gives ample evidence of the
directional retreat of the Ice Age, an age that is recent history
compared to where all the land came from.

About 180 million years ago, this ancient ocean floor consisted of assorted geological plates that got into a shoving match with the North American plate. It seems that some omnipotent scribe said to North America, "Go west, young man," and all hell broke loose. America's western edge advanced across the ocean bed, scraping up innocent islands as it moved, "plastering them onto the leading edge of the old continent," as Jim Monger puts it.

Before we get to Salt Spring, we have some mountains to take care of. This first continental advance piled volcanic rock atop the original crust and formed today's Interior mountains (between Revelstoke and Golden on Highway 1) before continuing west. The Big Scrape continued for another 90 million years as the western front picked up an assortment of geological goodies. It seems that a variety of exotic land masses were shifting about the pre-Pacific ocean and gradually drifted into North America. This material has been pegged at 180 to 400 million years old and was ultimately given the regional name Wrangellia (think Wrangell Mountains in southern Alaska, where similar rocks are found).

Harbour Air and Pacific Spirit Air seaplane services provide links to the mainland and also offer a great means to get an aerial view of Gulf Island geology.

Burgoyne Bay, a long-time logging ground, sits on the east side of the island, south of Sansum Narrows.

It is this rock mass that today underlies Vancouver Island, much of the southwestern mainland, and the southern third of Salt Spring Island. Mind you, the west coast was nowhere near Salt Spring at the time. In fact it was all part of the continental margin that extended from present-day Lytton to eastern Manning Park. After a few million years of bulking up, we got some more mountains in the region of Harrison Lake and the Fraser Canyon.

Even back then the area had its fair share of rain. Rain meant rivers, which meant erosion, which meant sand, gravel, mud, and deltas. These sediments were buried, then cemented by groundwater and heat to form sandstones, conglomerates, and shale that geologists now call the Nanaimo Group. It is this land mass that underlies most of the Gulf Islands including the northern two-thirds of Salt Spring.

This brings us to one of Mother Nature's great secrets. How could she possibly have known that long ago that Salt Spring was going to need some way to divide its two telephone exchanges? Yes, the 653 exchange serves Wrangellia and 537 serves the sandstone crowd (most locals will point out a few more distinctions between the southern folk and the northerners). The break serves to delineate Wrangellia from your basic North America.

About 50 million years ago there was a little more restlessness. The sandstone was folded, faulted, broken, and tilted—all in preparation for the invention of the camera. Majestic formations now blanket the shoreline around Georgia Strait.

Mountain building continued as the North American

plate plodded onward, steadily shoving more ocean floor beneath its mass into what is known as the *subduction* zone. (For *seduction* zone, look under accommodations.) Overall this endless onslaught buried 13,000 kilometres of ocean bed. Occasionally the subduction zone and molten rock core acted up and pushed their way through the advancing North American crust. The result was volcanoes if they reached the surface and massive pods of granite if they didn't. The former had a pleasant impact on today's landscape, creating such masterpieces as Mounts Garibaldi, Caley, and Meager in the Coast Mountains north of Squamish and Mount Baker in the Cascades of Washington state. It was likely Eastman Kodak that suggested adding a healthy dose of glacial ice and regular sprinklings of virgin snow in preparation for mankind's twentieth century.

Back to that 13,000 kilometre push westward—does it still occur? Jim Monger says, "The ocean floor dives beneath the western edge of the North American plate at a rate of 4.5 centimetres per year—at about the speed which fingernails grow." In other words, it's just a matter of time before Tokyo and Victoria are but a ferry ride apart.

Where does this dive take place? Almost close enough to be a tourist attraction. "Near the base of the continental slope, about 100 kilometres west of Vancouver Island in water depths of about 2000 metres," explains the geology professor. It is this relentless action and the resulting pressures that cause tremors and earthquakes.

So for millions of years there were two random land masses floating about, destined to snuggle up together in the Gulf of Georgia. As fate would have it, on Salt Spring the Wrangellian mass got dumped on by eras' worth of sediment and other upheavals. Then it took the Ice Age about two million years to get everything in order as we know it today. Using erosion, water, and ice as her sculpting implements and glacial activity as her bulldozer, Mother N got very creative. In the case of Salt Spring, she delivered the best of all worlds, leaving us both some bare Wrangellia and, to the north, a 4000-metre-deep layer of the Nanaimo Group components that evolved from very different geological activities. The best place to grasp this distinction is Mount Maxwell Park.

Mount Maxwell is a unique outcropping, isolated from but still part of the Nanaimo Lakes Highlands, which are primarily positioned on Vancouver Island. Maxwell likely originated as volcanic discharge somewhere in the south Pacific, but is now the western sentinel of Wrangellia and the Fulford Fault Line on Salt Spring. The fault line actually runs from Burgoyne Bay to Fulford Harbour, parallelling the main road. Bare Wrangellia runs from the mountain across the island just south of Cusheon Lake in a line fairly consistent with Kitchen Road. As mentioned, this line separates the 653s from the 537s of the telephone world. The Fulford Fault Line itself could be said to divide

EONS AND ERAS—THOSE WERE THE DAYS!

What is the best thing about a geology lesson? You finally get to learn the difference between an eon and an era. It turns out that regardless of how often the word appears in crossword puzzles, Earth has experienced only two eons—and one of those ended 590 million years ago, so it's hard to get worked up about. In case anybody does, it was the Precambrian Eon and it lasted about four billion years (that's American billion, not English billion).

The first eon was called Precambrian because it preceded the first period of the first era of the current eon, which coincidentally was called the Cambrian period. Geologists are very logical people. This eon, which could have simply been called the Second Eon according to my logic, is called the Phanerozoic eon and it has had three different eras. The oldest of these, the Paleozoic era, had six different periods, the earliest three of which are hardly relevant as Wrangellia was still just a gleam in the Era Maker's eye. Most geologists believe that Wrangellia was sidling toward North America during the youngest three Paleozoic periods: the Devonian, Carboniferous, and Permian periods. That era lasted 345 million years — and I thought the 1980s went on forever!

Next came the Mesozoic era, which had Triassic, Jurassic, and Cretaceous periods, at least one of which was so defined because we were running out of names for parks. Finally our era, the Cenozoic era, came along with its Tertiary period followed by the Quaternary period. Enough? Not quite. Being contemporary and all, it was time to create some epochs, namely what geologists call the Pleistocene epoch and normal people call the Ice Age. That ended 10,000 years ago with mucho melting, and we entered the Holocene or Recent epoch. Is it a brief respite before another freeze?

Wrangellia into two geological provinces. After glacial ice had done its face scrape here, the mass east of the fault was designated by geologists as the Salt Spring Intrusion. It is older than the mass to the far southwest of the island that includes Mount Tuam. West of the Fulford-Ganges Road, north of Tuam, the oldest formations slope upward to the island's highest point at 704 metres, Bruce Peak.

In a 1997 *Driftwood* article, Briony Penn wrote of historic clashes over the Salt Spring hunting ground between the Cowichan and Wsanec (Saanich) First Nations. Apparently they divided the land the same way the white folks settled on the telephone prefixes.

The sandstone of Southey Point, Vesuvius Beach, and the Ganges Harbour area is representative of the Nanaimo Lowland region. To a large extent the structural distinctions of south and north go back to the Big Scrape. In simple terms, the south end of the island got scraped a lot cleaner than the north, baring the soul of Wrangellia—more ancient rock formations, granites in particular. Mount Tuam was formed by layers of shale and slate settled through the ages. Beneath this mountain, softer slates, shales, and sediments were either removed completely or ground into glacial till as found in the Fulford Valley.

This valley and the soft formations that run from Ganges to the Booth Canal consist of sand, gravel, silt, and clay. Jim Monger says, "They may well have been the bed of ancient rivers and glacial melt."

The sediment layers on northern Salt Spring and most other Gulf Islands are up to four kilometres deep and are composed of sediment from the Coast and Cascade mountains.

SALT SPRING CONGENIALITY

In deference to things geological, many local residents have adopted two specific geological terms as part of their personality. *Erratics* in geological terms are boulders lifted from one area by glacial activity and deposited far from home. This description aptly applies to many island immigrants who have randomly descended upon us.

Likewise, land formations of unique makeup are sometimes called *unconformities*. Ferry passengers on the

Volcano on the Horizon

From many points on Salt Spring and surrounding islands, the majesty of Mount Baker, 120 kilometres distant, is a memorable sight on a clear day. This volcano last erupted in 1872 and is part of what is known as the Cascade magmatic arc. Such arcs form where geological plates meet—in this case the North American Plate and the subducting ocean floor, the Juan de Fuca Plate. The Cascade arc extends from Mount Garibaldi near Whistler, B.C., to Mount Shasta in northern California. Other members of this regal group are Mount Rainier, Mount Hood, and the remains of Mount St. Helens.

The conflicting forces of two plates moving in contrary directions drive the oceanic crust deeper, to the point where it melts. These molten materials, combined with volcanic pressure in the earth's core, have created an arc of release points where lava has penetrated the upper crust, forming volcanoes. The end result is ancient volcanic mountains and the occasional dramatic event, as witnessed in our lifetime in the eruption of Mount St. Helens.

route between the mainland and Vancouver Island can see such an unconformity along Beaver Point east of the Fulford Harbour entrance. There are some locals who might suggest that the entire social structure of Beaver Point is an unconformity, but geologists are referring to the unconventional layering of materials. At Beaver Point it seems that Cretaceous period sandstone lies next to deformed Paleozoic rock, and there is nothing Jurassic or Triassic in between. Because of this, residents and visitors alike are welcome to have a non-conforming picnic in nearby Ruckle Park.

Getting Serious

If you have a desire to know more about regional geology, a unique field guide by Chris Yorath and Hugh Nasmith may be of interest. *The Geology of Southern Vancouver Island* provides the entire lowdown on this fascinating science, with extensive detail on the Victoria area.

Questions and Answers

Are there fossils on Salt Spring?
Marine macro and trace fossils occur in both fine- and coarse-grained formations but are quite random on Salt Spring Island. Apparently biological life was too active for fossils to form. In other words, other creatures would eat or disturb dead biological specimens before they could fossilize. Fossils form in stagnant areas.

Where can I go to see different materials?
Conglomerates preserved on the top of Mount Maxwell represent the lowest layer of the Nanaimo Group—the Comox Formation. At Vesuvius Beach and the shore at Moby's Pub, shale beds are visible. Welbury Bay and Grace Point are formed by tipped-up sandstone. Channel Ridge is sandstone; Nose Point is conglomerate. All ridges on Salt Spring's north end are held up by sandstone and conglomerates. Erosion of soft shale beds can cause slides like that which covered North End Road along St. Mary Lake in December 1996.

How did glaciation affect Salt Spring?
Glaciation rounded off the tops of mountains and gouged out softer materials which formed St. Mary, Cusheon, and Weston Lakes, to name the largest. Jim Monger explained that Georgia Strait was already a depression created by the raising of forms on either side. The ice merely complemented this process. The impact of glaciation is with us today. Water shortages that can occur over much of the island are in some cases the result of sharp-edged, angular sandstone formations resisting the collection of water. Over time, groundwater has seeped between the sandstone particles and crystallized, much as tile grouting does when wet, forming an impermeable solid. As a result, when it rains, rather than seeping into the ground and being trapped, rainwater washes over the impermeable sandstone and eventually into the sea.

BETWEEN A ROCK AND A HARD PLACE

*Salt Spring, like many islands, is known for its local springtime passion
and a game of romance locally dubbed "The Salt Spring Shuffle." One
by-product of this game is the occasional tryst atop Mount Maxwell.
While many conclude that it is the view and the setting sun that prove
seductive, the real explanation may be more geological than just plain
logical. In the future, we suggest that any indiscretions committed here
should be blamed solely on the Fulford Fault.*

*And a word of warning to the romantics out there. One favoured
parking spot atop the mountain sits next to a series of three large
boulders. A small spaceship of alien voyeurs has occasionally been
rumoured to land behind the farthest stone. It is now known as "the third
rock from the sin."*

View of the Fulford Valley from the top of Mount Maxwell.

3

To Preserve & Protect

Government By the People, For the People

It's said that there are people who stood on different sides of the Ganges sewer issue back in the mid-1970s who still don't talk to each other. Various forces were at work and a localized Salt Spring "war" was underway. It was the classic clash between those who wanted more development and those who didn't. Interestingly, this battle started almost a century after the island's first great political battle (see *Early Politics*).

Salt Spring residents were in the midst of creating their first community plan, and many rural residents stood in opposition to the Ganges businesses that wanted to install a sewer system. When the Ganges forces moved ahead, a barge loaded with sewer pipe was mysteriously set ablaze in

EARLY POLITICS

It seems that politicians have always been in hot water on Salt Spring. In 1873, two years after B.C. entered Canada and five years after Salt Spring residents had elected their first representative to B.C.'s legislative assembly, the island was incorporated as the Township of Salt Spring. However, when the first elected council of seven started passing by-laws and defining taxes, all hell broke loose.

Many remote farmers, who saw themselves as the only source of tax money, immediately regretted signing the incorporation petition and sought relief. In an alignment that seems destined to last forever, early pro-developers were vehemently opposed by settlers who favoured a pastoral life. The battle raged for a decade and culminated in a lawsuit launched after the 1881 municipal election. By then a vast majority of rural farmers were dead against municipal politics. Eric Roberts wrote, "Pioneers who had lived together as brothers passed each other on the trail without a sign of recognition...The dispute tore apart the whole community."

Islanders did not like the idea of a ferry fare hike in 1997, so they decided to hold a demonstration. Inspired by another group of revolutionaries and the Boston Tea Party over 200 years earlier, Ken Lee, and a contingent of loyal protesters, get ready to throw a case of "tea" off the Fulford ferry ramp after pointing out that they, like the Bostonians, were being levied unfair tariffs by unknowing bureaucrats from across the sea.

Welbury Bay. This alleged arson has never been solved. The next barge came with armed guards and watchdogs.

The bonfire drew both media and political attention and eventually a special act of the B.C. legislature forced the island community to comply with the approved sewage plan.

The sewer war no doubt was a catalyst that expedited the passing of another piece of legislation. On May 21, 1974, James Lorimer, minister of Municipal Affairs for British Columbia, introduced the Islands Trust Act. After two weeks of debate, the act was passed and a unique new form of government was put in place to preserve and protect one of the most pristine and accessible island clusters in the world.

THE TRUST AREA

The Trust Area, as it is known, encompasses all islands and waters of the southern Strait of Georgia that are not covered by B.C. mainland or southern Vancouver Island communities and First Nations reserves. In addition to Salt Spring, there are 12 other major islands and 450 small islands governed by the Islands Trust.

It became apparent to an environmentally conscious public in the late 1960s that the Gulf Islands, home to more than 200 species of migratory and resident birds plus a diverse range of marine and terrestrial wildlife, needed protection from unrestrained development. Subdivision restrictions were put in place as the government made a concerted effort to promote community planning throughout the islands.

In an act of mutual concern and respect for their shared responsibility, Canada and the United States, in an international joint commission, acknowledged the need to preserve water quality, wildlife habitat, and historic and archaeological sites in both the Gulf and San Juan Islands. In 1973 this commission proposed that an international park be established, which further spurred governments to address the issues at hand.

The Islands Trust

Instead of a park, the provincial government, wanting more direct representation, placed the islands in a trust. Trustees would be appointed or elected with a mandate to preserve and protect the natural resources that existed, while also addressing the inevitable changes and problems caused by human population growth in the Trust Area. On that basis they became the primary authority on land-use issues and all rezoning applications within the Trust Area.

At first a council of three general trustees was appointed for a two-year term, to be responsible for all general policies. Each of the thirteen major islands was also represented by two local trustees more attuned to the concerns of their individual island. The main criticism of the legislation was that the three general trustees could overrule the local trustees, thereby denying residents of any given island the right to self-determination.

Residents of Salt Spring were pacified on this issue to a degree because one of the original three general trustees was local resident Marc Holmes, an apolitical environmentalist and twenty-year army veteran. Holmes, Hilary Brown of Hornby Island, and Dave Brousson of North Vancouver were appointed and made fully aware of their mandate. Section 3(1) of the Islands Trust Act read:

It is the object of the Trust to preserve and protect, in co-operation with the municipalities and the Government of the Province, the Trust Area and its unique amenities and environment for the benefit of the residents of the Trust Area and the Province generally.

In 1977, amendments to the Act ensured that a total of 26 trustees would be elected, two each from the thirteen larger islands. The Islands Trust was also given the power to develop and amend Trust Area community plans and zoning by-laws.

Although fought by some, the allocation of these powers was both timely and prudent. The Salt Spring sewer war and abuse of the lack of zoning restrictions had proven that bureaucracy had its place. By 1974, Salt Spring had developed its first community plan, and while it allowed some cluster development, green space was written into the formula. After 1977, that community plan was finalized and the island's role in self-government came down to the election of its two island trustees and plan implementation.

These trustees are now elected to serve three-year terms. Under the current system, all local land-zoning issues on a given island are addressed by a Trust committee made up of three trustees—two from the island in question and a third committee chairperson who comes from another island. The third member acts to protect the interest of other islands in matters that concern them. Collectively, all 26 trustees respond to issues that affect more than one jurisdiction.

The Islands Trust has always demanded that developers be ecologically responsible in their designs. In most cases, both trustees and those they serve would rather err on the side of conservation than establish a legacy of misallocation.

The Islands Trust matured as a political body over a twenty-year period, its successes far outweighing its controversies. On Salt Spring it had a somewhat shaky start because the Ganges sewer issue dominated local concern and the Islands Trust sat on the fence.

For the first decade, those who were elected tended to serve only for a single term, as the time demands were substantial and the financial rewards minimal. In the mid-1980s two support groups, the Advisory Planning Committee, appointed by local service organizations, and the Design Council, a volunteer group interested in maintaining the integrity of community design, were set up to aid the trustees. Recently these groups were joined by a third entity, the Advisory Transportation Committee.

On Salt Spring, the Trust's effectiveness is easily measured by the broad support given by the public. For the most part it has worked. Watersheds have been protected, waterfront development has been controlled, ribbon development along the main road has been avoided. On only one occasion did the structure prove ineffective. Two warring trustees, always in conflict, combined with an off-island chairperson unwilling to decide Salt Spring's destiny on key issues to produce a stalemate. One term of that was enough and may serve islanders well in the long run as they reflect on the importance of electing trustees who are able to resolve conflict.

The Islands Trust Act was redrafted in 1990. It assigned a new regional planning function to the Trust council. Population in the Trust Area grew 26 percent between 1986 and 1991. Ferry traffic was up 37 percent on inter-island routes. Summer tourist traffic was placing new demands on limited water supplies in some locations. Those trends have not changed. On Salt Spring there is talk of planning for the future.

THE TRUST ISLANDS

There are a total of 26 trustees elected to serve on the Islands Trust council for three-year terms. The thirteen major islands that individually elect two trustees each are: Bowen, Denman, Gabriola, Galiano, Hornby, Lasqueti, Mayne, North Pender, South Pender, Salt Spring, Saturna, Thetis, and Valdes.

A New Community Plan

Since 1995, many residents have committed themselves to the lengthy, complicated process of re-examining the status quo and helping define a new community plan. A first draft of the 1996 community plan, as presented by the Islands Trust, drew a broad and thunderous response and stimulated numerous public meetings.

Recent arrivals and some long-time residents got politically involved for the first time in their lives. Many property owners were outraged at proposed restrictions that constrained their individual rights. Others strongly against further development applauded the draft plan. The result was a second draft of the community plan, introduced only weeks before the 1996 election of Salt Spring's trustees.

Both Bob Andrew and Grace Byrne opted not to run for another term in 1996. The trustees elected, Bev Byron and David Borrowman, have moved this draft forward and it is expected to be adopted in 1998.

IN WHO WE TRUST

Bob Andrew was described by detractors as a Beaver Point whittler living in an old school bus. He was a small-framed man, a full, rust-coloured beard his dominant feature. His straw hat, bulky sweater, levis, heavy wool socks, and sandals were accepted as standard issue for the Fulford crowd. The year was 1990 and Bob, a talented artisan who worked primarily in wood, had just been elected as one of Salt Spring's two new trustees.

Based on appearance alone, there are few electorates in North America that would have supported this candidate in his first political venture. Over the next six years, Bob not only justified his supporters' confidence but also displayed knowledge, self-assurance, and vision that won him respect island-wide.

Bob recalls arriving on Salt Spring from the Prairies in 1980. "As soon as my feet touched the ground, I felt that I was in a magical, wonderful place," he says. With other family members, he soon settled on a new homestead on Beaver Point.

Bob befriended Nick Gilbert, who in the mid-1980s was chairman of the Islands Trust council. Under Nick's influence, Bob, a trained biologist, became more involved in community affairs and soon found himself appointed warden of the Mount Tuam ecological reserve. Bob was dead set against a B.C. Ferry Corporation plan to move the Fulford terminal to Isabella Point and in 1986 found himself a member of the Island Watch Society and a political activist.

After hearing the mandate of the Trust read at a meeting, he spoke his feelings publicly for the first time.

"Not only is the Islands Trust the only form of local government that I could become interested in; I could be in love with it." He reflected on his personal growth. "Little did I realize that I could become more and more enamoured with what the Trust is and what their council was mandated to achieve: Hold the lands in trust for the people of the islands and the people of B.C."

Recently, Bob expressed sincere appreciation that "somebody saw the light to slow down development in these beautiful, sensitive areas." Asked what the Trust has actually done, he answered, "It's not so much what they've done as it is what we have not seen happen over the years."

As we sat beside tranquil Fulford Harbour, Bob's thoughts turned to a substantial condo complex that had been proposed for the hillside, only to be rejected by the trustees. He also recalled how surprised he was at the support he had received from the newcomers he felt might stand against his cautious position on development. "Time and time again, the newest arrivals become very protective of this new home they have chosen. They know what happened to the places they left."

Among his electorate there was diverse perception of the issues and he says his biggest challenge was to find the common vision and protect it.

"The Trust mandate is defined by a policy statement, but it is people who define where we are going and what we are. Balance," he says. "The Trust strives to keep a balance between individual ideas of what is special about the islands and the real needs of the human condition."

The task of controlling development becomes even more difficult with population growth and the mindset of a consumer-driven society. Everyone has a slightly different idea of what modern amenities should be accommodated while maintaining the motto of "preserve and protect."

"In a small community like Salt Spring, you are forced to listen to the people," he observes. "If you don't listen, they will kick you out."

Bob listened, and the sincerity of his love of Salt Spring was never in doubt. "Once land is overdeveloped or clear-cut, it can't be undone," he says.

Bob played a large role in developing Salt Spring's new

Bob Andrew and Grace Byrne at their farewell party from the Trust, February 1997.

community plan, presenting the first draft in 1996. There was great controversy and his real strengths became visible as the outcry grew. Staying with the project, Bob listened carefully to valid concerns articulated by all sides and he worked hard to redraft a plan to reflect the people's wishes. As we write, that plan stands ready to become the future for Salt Spring.

Bob Andrew will be remembered as a fair, honest man who stood by his own beliefs and has done his bit to keep Salt Spring "a magical wonderful place to be."

Grace Byrne and husband Pat moved to Salt Spring in 1983 from Canmore, Alberta, to enjoy a more moderate climate and pursue their gardening interests. No stranger to community service, Grace had served on the Canmore school board for seven years.

Embracing her new home, Grace was elected to the local school board and was the board's representative on the Advisory Planning Committee before 1993. In that year she joined Bob Andrew as an Islands Trust trustee. For Grace, Salt Spring is "a special place not just for the people who live here, but for all B.C.ers to enjoy."

Commenting on the Trust as a form of government, Grace says, "We've been recognized as being very special and unique." She devoted endless hours to developing the new community plan, but sees her most important accomplishment as stopping the attempt to dump contaminated material dredged from Ganges Harbour in an island watershed. "If the dredgings were not good enough for fish, they are not good enough for a watershed," she concluded.

Along with refining the community plan and continuing the work of producing improved land-use by-laws, Grace hopes future trustees can get more Crown land designated for parks. "I think more hiking and walking trails are one of the nicest things we can do for our own people, visitors, and the tourist industry," she offers as a final remark.

Grace was a trustee with strong convictions and the courage of her convictions. During a three-year term she earned respect and served her island well.

As architects of the first draft of a new community plan, the 1993-96 trustees stimulated a new era in island politics. The controversy that surrounded that draft plan led to eight candidates seeking the two trustee positions in the 1996 election. Such political involvement was new for many islanders and the debate was heated. Campaign promises ranged from pro-development to no-development. "Bust the Trust" was the war cry of one faction.

Leading the polls was **Bev Byron**, a retired teacher. Given her reputation as a teacher and as a woman of practicality, her popularity was not surprising. The Byrons had first homesteaded on Salt Spring during the Great Depression, and Bev brought a moderate, historic perspective to the forum. She felt "a need to represent working people, to offset the environmentalist lobby, to represent the business community—a need to make sure the views and interests of the economic community were represented."

Bev had entered the race after being recruited by supporters and was an inexperienced politician. "I had no idea how complicated issues can be," she mused. While she considers herself pro-environment, she says, "We must protect the people who own the land. It's theirs, they bought it, and you can't take it away from them. It must be a 50-50 deal. You can't go whole hog, one way or the other."

Bev says that one of her main problems deals with short-sighted zoning rules brought in 25 years ago. "When they set up zoning, they simply zoned property based on its use at the time. A small sawmill amidst a residential cluster was zoned industrial. We face the ramifications of patchwork zoning every day."

A conciliator at heart, Bev sees endorsement of a sound community plan and a true meeting of the minds as key goals during the rest of her term. Addressing zoning quirks and liquid sewage issues is impossible until that is achieved. In the trustee job, Bev may have bitten off more than she expected, but she is willing to chew as needed.

With many former students among her constituents, Bev continues to teach them responsibility, loyalty, and commitment through her own actions.

The second trustee currently representing Salt Spring on the Islands Trust is **David Borrowman**.

Following a lengthy career in the Canadian Foreign Service, David retired from his posting as Canada's Consul in Oslo, Norway. During his days as a diplomat, David had long dreamed of building a log home in a quiet, secluded setting. He searched the United States, Australia, and a large part of Canada before coming to visit a friend on Salt Spring Island. Arriving in Long Harbour by ferry on a dark, rainy October night, David immediately sensed he had finally found his new home.

"I felt the connection and wanted to be here," he recalls. Enthralled by the sociability of the place, he says, "I found myself surrounded by many more like-minded people and interesting people than I ever knew in government, even in a city the size of Ottawa."

He has served his community in many capacities, including as an Advisory Planning commissioner and a contributor to a study of local government options. Drawn into the politics of the proposed plan, he decided to stand for election as a trustee in November 1996.

His personal view is that the Gulf Islands will always need the Trust in some form. "One municipality government could do tremendous damage without any outside control. In my view, that control should be the Trust. One ill-conceived town zoning decision could create tremendous harm that you'd never recover from. We can conserve land for years and years, but once it is built on, that's the end of it."

This packed hall at a 1990 community meeting reflects both the willingness of locals to get involved and their ability to set aside the issue long enough for a good laugh.

David explains the makeup of the Islands Trust was never intended to be representation by population. It was set up as a federation, and "if the federation works properly, big guys take care of the little guys and they recognize the big guy's interests."

Many islanders continue to feel that Salt Spring Island should have increased representation because of its population and because it is the largest of all the Gulf Islands. They see it as unfair that a population approaching 10,000 is represented by only two trustees—the same as an island

INFLATION ON SALT SPRING

Land prices on Salt Spring were not the same problem in the nineteenth century that they became in this century. Copland's original deal with Governor Douglas said that the eventual price of pre-empted land, once it was surveyed, would be no more than $1.25 per acre. The going rate in the 1880s when the Mouats settled was about one dollar per acre. Richard P. E. Roberts paid the same in 1896 for 157 acres. His property changed hands twice and was sold for five thousand dollars in 1907. It was only the beginning!

as small as Thetis with only hundreds of residents. However, David feels Salt Spring is being quite well served by the federation. He is more concerned about the organization's structure at a local level. When two locally elected trustees are at odds, it is the chairperson of the Trust Council, someone from a neutral island, who makes a final decision affecting Salt Spring Island.

Although he thinks the Trust as a whole works well and has achieved some major accomplishments, he cites the following failures. "I feel we are playing catch-up regarding the environment. No stream is in good enough shape. We have a great restoration job to be done; we haven't anticipated these things properly."

David sees the Trust's biggest challenge as making sure there are some benefits to landowners so they do not give in to development. "We need tax benefits for people who are preserving their land as green space."

David expresses his dedication to the "preserve and protect mandate" of the Islands Trust this way: "As a man who has visited thirty-two countries and lived abroad for extended periods of time, I find it hard to overstate my estimation of the beauty and the intactness of the islands on a world scale. They're worth preserving simply by definition."

So You Want To Live On Salt Spring?

Salt Spring is no longer an inexpensive place to live. Although property values have stabilized in recent years, waterfront continues to be in high demand and is priced accordingly. There are a few condominium clusters, like Grace Point in Ganges, and subdivisions, such as Channel Ridge, Hundred Hills, and Ganges Village. However the average lot size on much of the island is five acres.

If you have bought or are thinking of buying land on Salt Spring, we strongly advise you to visit the Islands Trust office in Ganges to take a look at the zoning by-laws so you know what you can and cannot do with the land.

Water supply is another matter to consider if you dream of living on Salt Spring. A few areas are on a common water system, but most properties obtain their water from wells or underground springs. Although Ganges and part of Fulford Village are on sewer systems, all other individual properties must have either chemical treatment plants or septic systems. If you are buying raw land, your offer to purchase should be subject to a perc test and approval issued by the Capital Regional District (CRD), which looks after servicing, e.g., building permits, septic systems, etc.

Natural gas is not yet available, so electricity, propane, oil, and wood-burning stoves are the prime sources of residential heat.

Taxes on the island are relatively low compared to many places, but services are limited. Garbage disposal is handled by three private companies and you pay for garbage pickup by the bag.

On Salt Spring, parcels of land three acres or larger are zoned to allow residents to build a 600-square-foot guest cottage in addition to their home. These are a popular investment. If you choose to move to Salt Spring, "company's coming" may have a whole new meaning in your life. Remember how much you liked the island as a visitor—all your friends and relatives will feel the same way and will be delighted to visit you. A guest cottage may be your salvation.

Many people start looking for property with a southern exposure, but because its availability is limited and because many of the most spectacular views are to the east, people quickly adjust. Buyers tend to fall in love with either the house or the property/location and then adjust their wish list accordingly. Price is always a factor, but surprisingly, a number of realtors say it is often not the prime concern. Retirement buyers coming from an urban setting look at

View from Vesuvius looking across to Vancouver Island.

REAL ESTATE ON SALT SPRING

Every year, hundreds of visitors who discover Salt Spring Island leave reluctantly, believing they have found their dream—a perfect place to escape to or to call home. Many people are barely into their second day on the island before they start looking for their prize piece of this world. It's easy to enlist the aid of a real estate agent. Salt Spring has over 40 serious sales reps from numerous established agencies including Remax, and Windermere. According to Russ Crouse, a long-time realtor on Salt Spring, "lifestyle is the major draw for newcomers."

Because it is so easy to be swept up in the beauty, the carefree atmosphere, and the friendliness of the people, responsible realtors suggest that prospective buyers visit the island at least three times before making this major decision. We suggest they consider renting for a minimum of three to six months and spend a winter on the island before they purchase. It's a great place to be while in holiday mode, but life changes considerably if you need to make a living here.

their home as a lifestyle decision. They want something they really like and are going to feel comfortable living in.

Many people decide to move here and then figure out how they can make it work for them. It's one of the reasons why the island is home to so many creative entrepreneurs. Home-based businesses are very common and the zoning by-laws encourage this type of enterprise. As a result, many prospective buyers look for properties with office, studio, or workshop options—not to mention space for a B&B.

Salt Spring, like all places, has a few "neighbourhoods." Those most comfortable in an "upscale" setting should look to the Sunset Drive, Reginald Hill, Southey Point area or to Scott Road near Long Harbour.

While much of the development has been north of our own Mason/Dixon Line (also identified as Kitchen Road, the faultline, or the 537/653 line), many people find the south end more appealing.

The best advice we can offer is to explore everywhere, take a bit of time with your decision, but once you've made it, embrace your future with passion!

Tom Grundy and his horses begin a hayride from downtown Ganges.

Santa Claus arrives by seaplane.

The Polar Bear Swim is an annual New Year's Day event that even attracts zebras.

Local artist Lorraine Sullivan with one of her paintings at Pegasus Gallery.

4

A Colony of Cultural Arts

And 1000 Lifestyles

SALT SPRING'S CULTURAL PERSONA DEFIES DESCRIPTION—but we must try. On the surface it still appears to be a secret to the outside world. A recent survey suggested that only three percent of visitors were attracted to Salt Spring for cultural reasons. On the other hand, one U.S. publication recently included it in the top 100 art colonies of North America. With its cultural diversity and the audience such an environment attracts come a horde of liberal thinkers. And with such thinkers come a wide range of lifestyles.

Salt Spring's 10,000 residents take great pride in the creative element of their community, be it the work of established professionals or the efforts of amateur hobbyists and aspiring street performers. While many of the island's artisans work year-round to fill the summer tourist demand for their crafts, some painters use the island solely as their creative base and sell their work through major galleries around the world. International art stars like wildlife artist Robert Bateman actively participate in the local scene and support the development of the cultural community.

The current crop of artists and artisans has given Salt Spring a cultural reputation that has blossomed dramatically in the last quarter century, but the foundation for the island's endless variety of lifestyles goes back to its original settlers. From the earliest black and Kanaka communities of the 1860s and '70s to the "hippie invasion" a century later, Salt Spring has adopted a live-and-let-live attitude to most people and philosophies. It is a place where freedom and cultural expression are soul mates. Franklin Roosevelt once said, "Art cannot thrive except where men [and women] are free to be themselves." Salt Spring has proven that where freedom reigns, art does follow.

Much of the island's cultural growth can be traced back to the origins of the Community Arts Council and the distinctive system of craft guilds that were formed after 1968. Canada's country-wide surge of nationalism after the 1967 centennial celebrations led the provincial government to announce new funding support for the arts. One of the founders of the Arts Council was long-time resident Olive Clayton, who recently recalled how the craft groups came to exist. Names fondly remembered included Emily Crosby, Nita Brown, and Ruth Stanton.

"Ruth Stanton [now in her 90s] had always been a weaver and had started the handicraft guild in Yellowknife," Olive reminisced. "We started the Community Arts Council in 1968 and the guilds applied to CAC for funding."

The arts council administered the funds. "Nita was the first CAC president. Emily and Ruth established the guilds." The potters followed the weavers, she remembered. "The painters were the last to get organized. Nita recruited Winsor Utley, the man who built the castle down on Beddis Beach, to be the first Painter's Guild president."

With its formation, the arts council initiated the Summer Artcraft Show, an exhibition that has since become an annual tradition on Salt Spring. The show moved to Ganges' Mahon Hall in 1980 after the building was restored. Olive remembers Mahon Hall as "a grungy old place," but is now content that thirty years after she first saw it, "it looks a lot better."

Guilds of jewellers, woodworkers, and fabric artists emerged with time. Olive noted that as the community grew, individuality often re-emerged and some of the guilds fragmented, though they still play an integral role in the island's cultural community.

Artisans continue to join the guilds as they provide both instruction and camaraderie for their members. Membership is much more casual than in the traditional guilds of Europe, but the groups—the painters, the weavers and spinners, the potters, the woodworkers, the jewellers, the Fabric Guild, and the "unguilded" Salt Spring Players—provide moral support and training to all comers. Collectively, over 200 guild members participate in Artcraft, June to mid-September from 10 til 5 daily, and at spring and pre-Christmas shows.

LOCALS AT LARGE

1. Raging grannies
2. Hang-glider off Mount Bruce
3. Valdy flogs the folk club
4. The tragically hick
5. Ganges Saturday market
6. Fall fair sheep trials
7. Damaris Rumsby's step class
8. Clamming at low tide
9. The Barley brothers
10. Kayakers in Ganges Harbour

Valdy and Friends entertaining at the annual Fulford Inn Christmas singalong.

It is the February event, however, that has become the hottest exhibition of the year: an Erotica Festival art show where a variety of visual excesses, from the sculpture to adults-only plays staged at festival time, warm up the local waters.

Like the residents of most remote communities, Salt Springers take pride in local characteristics, be they eccentric or practical. Locals have a keen eye, able at a glance to separate residents from tourists. Respect is given to many of the founding elders and, to a lesser extent, the offspring of those islanders who can trace their lineage back to some of the original families. However, with a growing number of the 1970s invaders now worthy of their twenty-year gumboot pins, that segment has become most associated with the island's art institutions.

The island's cultural events calendar is crammed during the summer months when tourists from across Canada and around the world descend on the Gulf Islands. The July Festival of Arts usually includes performances by the Hysterical Society and other theatre groups. Off-island entertainers join the festivities to the delight of locals and visitors alike. Many come because they love to be on Salt Spring. The concerts range from classical to rock and roll to jazz, blues, and folk.

Speaking of folk, Canadian folk legend Valdy (born Valdemar Horsdal) is a Salt Spring original and active participant in community life. He performs throughout the year at local pubs and for various fund-raising events. In 1998 he and Bill Henderson, another B.C. music legend, kicked off the second season of the Salt Spring Folk Club's fall/winter program with a performance by singer/songwriter Murray McLauchlan. The club imports international artists who would normally only be seen in venues larger than Salt Spring's durable (if not pretty) Fulford Hall.

Local groups who perform regularly include Ray and Virginia Newman, Auntie Kate, the Barley Brothers and the Stack Sisters. Kenny Byron's Tragically Hick is a western band that claims among its members the editor of the *Gulf Islands Driftwood*, Tony Richards. Salt Spring and Swing, a jazz combo, and Simone Gratsky (she brings back memories of Billie Holiday or Sarah Vaughan) often appear at Moby's or other venues. Unlike many places where the audience sits and listens to live music, here they dance the night away. "The first time I came to the island, I literally danced my

HOMEMADE JUICE AND MARGARET

"There was usually about twenty of us. Once all the wooden folding chairs were in place, Margaret would sit at the piano playing her tunes while the projectionist displayed home slides on the screen. There was always one slide of Margaret at the piano and on cue, when her slide appeared, Margaret would raise an arm, turn toward the audience, and give us a wave. She was like royalty."

Margaret Cunningham and her piano are part of Salt Spring's heritage.

Cathy Mack recalls those days on Salt Spring when the Central Theatre was a social crossroads of the island.

Margaret is Margaret Cunningham, the grand lady of the Cunningham homestead, Church Hill Farm, which still stands next door to the Central Community Hall that includes the theatre. Margaret was the piano teacher to many of the north island's youth for decades. Eventually she moved to Greenwoods, the island's seniors home.

"There was always home-pressed apple juice and fresh popcorn with engevita yeast. I can't remember the movies at all," Cathy reminisces. "But I'll always remember Margaret."

Now known simply as Central, this is the site of Central Settlement, where the island's first church and schoolhouse was a debarked log cabin built in 1861. The building itself dates back to the turn of the century when it was constructed as the island's first community hall. Given the century plus of good times and good vibes that have unfolded here, some think that the music of Margaret Cunningham and the spirit of the first schoolteacher, John C. Jones, still linger in the rafters.

socks off," recalls Cathy Mack, a late 1970s arrival from the east. It was at the Harbour House Hotel, and the energy was infectious. She is nostalgic about the memory. "I danced to the sounds of Club Mongo for five hours straight," she says.

Salt Spring choral groups performing through the year include Salt Spring Singers and Tuned Air. In July, Tuned Air has an annual wine-tasting fund-raiser that combines the best of B.C. and international wineries with performances by the group. Wine enthusiast Steve Coopman offers a monthly Wine Tasting and Art Show at Thunderbird Gallery, with the current show's artist in attendance. Catch Steve's monthly wine column in the *Driftwood*.

Live theatre productions on Salt Spring range from amateur to professional, the only constant being enthusiasm. A players group first formed in 1971, and now there are seven separate performing groups active on Salt Spring.

Amongst the best-known and most enthusiastic are the Raging Grannies, an amorphous band of dynamic dames who like to entertain and raise environmental awareness at the same time, Off Centre Stage, Active P.A.S.S. (Performing Artists of Salt Spring), and the Hysterical Society. The latter is a home-grown comedy troupe that has spent more

HOW TO BECOME A RAGING GRANNY

If retirement leaves a woman with a sense of restlessness, on Salt Spring there is always one option to consider. If you meet the standards, you can become a Raging Granny. The Grannies don't run a closed shop. All you need is a desire to save the world. There is no age limit and you do not have to be a grandmother to join although not a necessary prerequisite, it is a good idea to take along an outgoing personality. These gals pull no punches. Seriously interested in the future of life on earth, they select a weekly issue and protest every Saturday, belting out songs written by Betty Gibson's husband, Andy. He writes mainly local issue songs, and the women perform them at visible venues or target sites.

Raging Grannies are not indigenous to Salt Spring but are active all across Canada, the result of an uprising that started in Victoria ten years ago. The Grannies participate in street theatre, community education, and protesting. Local recruiting officer is Virginia Newman, 250-537-9251.

than a decade helping the community laugh at itself. Arvid Chalmers recalls how it took ten years of island living before he was able to overcome innate shyness and get up on stage. "I had just turned forty," he recalls, "and attended my first Off Centre Stage open comedy night." Finding it both funny and forgiving to the amateur performers, Arvid composed his own routine. "It was a seven-minute routine on my vasectomy. The audience really liked it and I got hooked." Arvid and a group of other open stage

Some of the original members of the Hysterical Society, Arvid Chalmers, Sheri Nielson, Anne Lyon, and James Wilkinson, in their highly successful play, Paradise Lots.

regulars soon formed the Hysterical Society. Readers Theatre, a group of people who act through their voices, performs once or twice a year.

The various companies use both community players and the smattering of professionally trained actors and directors who have managed to escape to a life on Salt Spring.

The theatre scene has not been without controversy. Fund-raising efforts to complete a theatre and visual arts centre have been underway for years. An attractive building called Artspring sits idle and unfinished in Ganges as organizers fight to meet the insatiable demand of the construction budget. When completed, Artspring will feature a 265-seat performance hall and 520 square metres of exhibition and classroom space. Until the centre is completed, most performances take place in Ganges elementary school, Mahon Hall, or other island venues like Fulford Hall and Beaver Point Hall.

Salt Spring's lone movie theatre is located in Central Hall. A mecca for local movie buffs, it's a cozy room replete with plush red seats and great popcorn. The theatre has a long and quaint history (see *Homemade Juice and Margaret*). Currently two movies are shown nightly and they change every three days. There is also an annual Film Festival; check the blackboard outside the theatre for details.

Local painter in downtown Ganges.

Salt Spring is a wonderful place to find quality local arts and crafts. Ganges and Fulford Harbour have retail galleries that sell paintings, photographs, wooden crafts, pottery, weavings, jewellery, and sculpture by local artists and artisans. Other locally crafted goods include dried flower creations, candles, natural soaps and lotions, metalwork, handmade papers, papiermâché masks, stained glass, and handcrafted board game replicas (like chess sets). These items can often be purchased in the studio shops that dot the island. Many are part of the

GALLERIES, SHOPS, AND MORE

It is impossible to keep up with newer locales, but there are some long-time favourites. North of Ganges, Foxglove *is more than a garden store, full of charming and colourful ideas. Further north,* Fraser Thimble Farms *at Southey Point and* The Plant Farm *on Vesuvius Bay Road are havens for gardeners and are particularly known for their wide range of ornamentals.*

The road to Ruckle Park passes McLennan Drive, where Everlasting Summer, *a dried-flower and herb farm earns rave reviews. In Fulford check out* Stuff & Nonsense *and* Tom Graham Pottery. *Ganges galleries and studios worth a visit include* Pegasus Gallery of Canadian Art *(Mouat's Mall),* Thunderbird, Naiki *(Grace Point Square),* Waterfront *(next to the post office), and* Jill Louise Campbell Gallery *(Harbour Building).* The Sophisticated Cow, *a wonderful collection of island treasures displayed in a heritage home, is a must see! Book enthusiasts will enjoy browsing in* Volume II, Island Books Plus Art Gallery *and* et cetera. West of the Moon *is an incredible toy store, loved by all ages!* Harlan's *is a chocoholic dream.* Love My Kitchen, The Tangled Web Knitting Studio, *and* Salt Spring Soapworks *are all worth a visit.* Ewart Gallery, *on Salt Spring Way just south of Ganges, is a long-established gallery that often hosts special exhibits.*

Fall Fair is one of the most popular events of the year.

Everlasting Summer *has a studio full of dried flower arrangements and a herb garden to wander through.*

Stuff & Nonsense *and* Tom Graham Pottery *in Fulford have a real sound end flavour.*

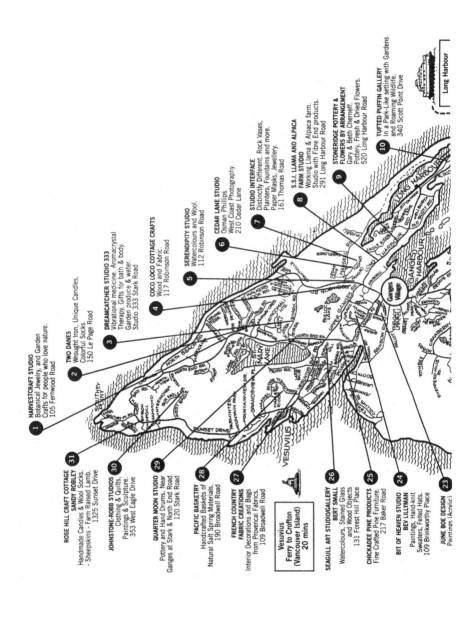

1 HARVESTCRAFT STUDIO
Botanical Jewelry, and Garden
Crafts for people who love nature.
105 Fernwood Road

2 TWO DANES
Wrought Iron, Unique Candles,
Colorful Socks.
150 Le Page Road

3 DREAMCATCHER STUDIO 333
Vibrational medicine. Aromacrystal
Therapy. Gifts for bath & body.
Garden produce & water.
Studio 333 Stark Road

4 COCO LOCO COTTAGE CRAFTS
Wood and Fabric.
117 Robinson Road

5 SERENDIPITY STUDIO
Watercolours and Wool.
112 Robinson Road

6 CEDAR LANE STUDIO
Osman Phillips.
West Coast Photography.
210 Cedar Lane

7 STUDIO INTERFACE
Distinctly Different. Rock Vases,
Planters, Fountains and more.
161 Thomas Road

8 S.S.I. LLAMA AND ALPACA FARM STUDIO
Working Llama & Alpaca farm.
Studio with Fibre End products.
291 Long Harbour Road

9 STONERIDGE POTTERY & FLOWERS BY ARRANGEMENT
Gary & Beth Cherneff.
Pottery, Fresh & Dried Flowers.
520 Long Harbour Road

10 TUFTED PUFFIN GALLERY
In a Park-Like setting with Gardens
and Roaming Wildlife.
340 Scott Point Drive

31 ROSE HILL CRAFT COTTAGE SANDY ROBLEY
Handmade Candles & Wool Socks.
- Sheepskins - Farm Raised Lamb.
1325 Sunset Drive

30 JOHNSTONE-ROBB STUDIOS
Clothing & Quilts,
Paintings & Sculpture.
353 West Eagle Drive

29 QUARTER MOON STUDIO
Pottery and Hand Drums. Near
Ganges at Stark & North End Road
120 Stark Road

28 PACIFIC BASKETRY
Handcrafted Baskets of
Natural Salt Spring Materials.
190 Broadwell Road

27 FRENCH COUNTRY FABRIC CREATIONS
Interior Decorations and Bags
from Provencal Fabrics.
109 Broadwell Road

26 SEAGULL ART STUDIO GALLERY BERT SMALL
Watercolours, Stained Glass
and Wood Objects
131 Forest Hill Place

25 CHICKADEE PINE PRODUCTS
Fine Crafted Pine Furniture.
217 Baker Road

24 BIT OF HEAVEN STUDIO BEV LILLYMAN
Paintings, Hand-knit
Sweaters, Felted Hats.
109 Brinkworthy Place

23 JUNE BOE DESIGN
Paintings (Acrylic)

Vesuvius
Ferry to Crofton
(Vancouver Island)
20 mins

Long Harbour

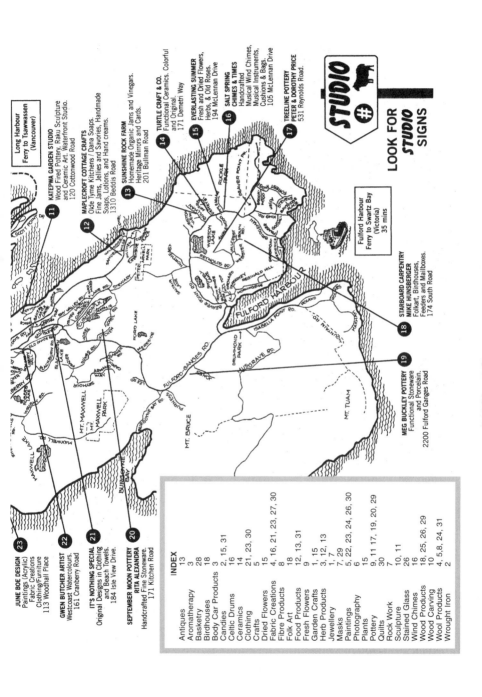

Long Harbour
Ferry to Tsawwassen
(Vancouver)

(11) KATEPWA GARDEN STUDIO
Wood Fired Pottery, Raku Sculpture
and Ceramic Art. Waterfront Studio.
120 Cottonwood Road

(12) MAPLECROFT COTTAGE CRAFTS
Olde Tyme Kitchens / Dana Soaps.
Fine Jams, Jellies and Savories. Handmade
Soaps, Lotions, and Hand creams.
1310 Beddis Road

(13) SUNSHINE ROCK FARM
Homemade Organic Jams and Vinegars.
Heritage Mirrors and Cards.
201 Bullman Road

(14) TURTLE CRAFT & CO.
Functional Ceramics. Colorful
and Original.
171 Demetri Way

(15) EVERLASTING SUMMER
Fresh and Dried Flowers,
Herbs, & Old Roses.
194 McLennan Drive

(16) SALT SPRING CHIMES & TIMES
Handcrafted
Musical Wind Chimes,
Musical Instruments,
Cushions & Bags.
105 McLennan Drive

(17) TREELINE POTTERY
PETER & DOROTHY PRICE
531 Reynolds Road.

STUDIO #

LOOK FOR
STUDIO
SIGNS

Fulford Harbour
Ferry to Swartz Bay
(Victoria)
35 mins

(18) STARBOARD CARPENTRY
MIKE HUNSBERGER
Folkart, Birdhouses,
Feeders and Mailboxes.
174 South Road

(19) MEG BUCKLEY POTTERY
Functional Stoneware
and Porcelain.
2200 Fulford Ganges Road

(23) JUNE BOE DESIGN
Paintings (Acrylic)
Fabric Creations
Clothing/Furniture
113 Woodhall Place

(22) GWEN BUTCHER ARTIST
Westcoast Watercolours.
161 Cranberry Road

(21) IT'S NOTHING SPECIAL.
Original Designs in Clothing
and Beach Towels.
184 Isle View Drive.

(20) SEPTEMBER MOON POTTERY
RITA ALEXANDRA
Handcrafted Fine Stoneware.
171 Kitchen Road

Studio Tour Map program, an annual participatory project involving studios that agree to receive visitors during set hours and jointly contribute to the map's production. The Studio Tour Map provides an ideal circuit for a day of discovery on the island. It is available in the Information Centre and from many businesses and accommodations operators. The map displays the locations of over 30 artisans. White, numbered, sheep posts at the entrance or turn-off to the studio make it easy to identify studio sites. Other independent artisans put up signboards on the roadways to indicate the hours when they will receive visitors.

The many unique farms on the island also contribute to the Salt Spring lifestyle and culture. Farmers grow a plethora of vegetables and fruit. Local grocery stores sell this produce or you can stop at one of the local farm stands dotted along island roads and buy direct. Defying urban trends, these stands often work on the honour system. When no one is minding the stand, you figure out your cost and make your own change from the money jar. It's enough to restore faith in humanity for some visitors.

Many island B&Bs pay tribute to local produce by incorporating it into their menus, and visitors to the island who stay in kitchen-equipped resorts or suites are assured of local ingredients all year long.

Gourmets searching for local treasuers must seek out the goat cheese of Toronto transplant David Wood. Famous in Ontario as a purveyor of fine food, David and his wife Nancy came to Salt Spring in 1990. He says, "We have a lot more parties than we ever had in Toronto. And the [former] billiards room is just right for Scottish country dancing."

Fresh and natural foods are a way of life on Salt Spring. Home gardens are the norm and organic growers offer their produce and recipes weekly at the Saturday markets in Ganges and Fulford. Any time from spring through late fall you could happen upon a number of tasty, edible, wild mushrooms. As local mycologist Victoria Olchowecki advises, "Garlic added to any wild mushroom makes it taste more like itself." Succulent wild blackberries can be picked from country lanes in August and September to be made into a delicious pie or crumble. Free-range eggs, local breads, honey purchased from David Harris, the sociable honeymaker on the Fulford-Ganges Road, local fruits and nuts in season—all are common last-day purchases for visitors heading home from the island who want a small consumable memento of their visit.

The island abounds with great seafood and meats. The local lamb is legendary, and hidden coves and harbours still yield clams, mussels (beware of "red tide" restrictions), and crabs. Two fresh fish stores in Ganges and an evergrowing list of seafood on restaurant menus make it easy to sample the fruits of local waters.

The third weekend in September is Fall Fair weekend at the Farmers' Institute on Rainbow Road. It's a chance for city dwellers and country cousins to see the best of island produce displayed for competition. And everyone plays a strange game called "cow pie bingo." The old-time atmosphere includes sheepdog competitions, a corn roast, a dunk tank, and plenty of mouth-watering food. This Farmers' Institute is the oldest in B.C. and is dedicated to the preservation of island heritage.

COW PIE BINGO

One of the early attractions at the Fall Fair is an empty field. This innocent-looking layout has only one oddity; a chalked or taped grid of checkerboard squares covers the area. Early on fair day, locals can be seen measuring the grade, testing the wind, checking the barometer, and conjuring up their own visions of the near future as they survey the fenced rectangle.

Eventually they sidle up to the selection booth and acquire their small piece of land, one of the 400 to 600 squares in the field. Squares are snapped up quickly as all takers await the grand entry of this year's "Queen Cow for a Day." Well-fed, content, and ready for anywhere from fifteen minutes to hours of fame, the cow is encouraged to roam the field at random. On the perimeter, entranced audience members try every method to entice the animal toward their square of real estate.

Over the years, eyes have stayed glued to the spectacle for up to eight hours. Why? The square that receives the first cow pie (feces bovinus for the literary crowd) determines the winner of a big pot of money.

HEALING ARTS

Given the above description of island life, it is hard to think of people needing soothing here, but there are many who see Salt Spring as a health oasis. Of the many methods of pain and stress reduction, perhaps the most avant-garde is the Swedan massage provided at the Salt Spring Centre for the Creative and Healing Arts. Swedan, an ancient ayurvedic treatment from India, is marketed as "a purifying and balancing balsam steam bodywork session...to relax the body and ease the mind." If you are intent on pampering yourself, opt for a 45-minute, full-body massage, then enter a sweat box garnished with aromatic boughs. As your body succumbs to the cleansing process, you are left feeling positively euphoric. Then barley flour is rubbed on your body with a stiff brush to remove dead cells from the surface of the skin. If you haven't had enough, you can move on to the centre's organic flower facial.

In recent years, Salt Spring has become the home of a wide range of therapy havens catering to a variety of contemporary ailments.

Stuart Katz and Doris Neufeld practise ancient Hawaiian Temple techniques used by Hawaiian Kahunas for

View out of Ganges Harbour from Moby's Pub.

spiritual, emotional, and physical healing. They also teach yoga and give massages.

Astha Bollinger offers acupressure and Masayo Hora is a practitioner of Cranio-Sacral Therapy as well as many other massage therapies. Cranio-Sacral Therapy influences the contents of the cranium and spinal column by altering the tension and mobility of the dural membrane system (internal lining of the spinal cord), using the bones of the cranium and sacrum as handles. Judith at Skin Sensations offers facials and waxing at her lovely waterfront location right in Grace Point Square in Ganges. In addition there are naturopathic physicians, therapeutic touch sessions, homeopathy, acupuncturists, aroma therapists, and Keldenkais practitioners, all helping to eliminate the effects of life's stresses and strains.

Appointments for treatment should be pre-booked by telephone.

Like any community, Salt Spring's population is made up of a mixture of age groups and socio-economic elements. Recently, the biggest migrating group has been retirees who come to enjoy the temperate climate of the Gulf Islands. Because Salt Spring has its own hospital and emergency helicopter service to a larger hospital in Duncan, seniors feel more secure here than on some of the less-developed islands. Health care, lifestyle, and a vibrant cultural diversity seem to be what a lot of people are seeking these days.

THE FOOD SCENE

It is in its food emporiums that many islanders first meet and quickly learn that dining attire, for the most part, is casual. It may take a while for some, but new residents, weekenders, and repeat visitors learn to mix and mingle on an island with very little class consciousness. The standard line is, "The millionaires come to town in their gumboots just like everyone else."

As elsewhere, restaurants come and go on Salt Spring, but year-round, from Vesuvius to Fulford Harbour, you can find flavourful meals.

Salt Spring's pubs, led by Moby's in Ganges, have developed a pretty good reputation for food in recent years.

The Vesuvius Inn and the Harbour House Bistro both have their fans. The Fulford Inn has a history of ups and downs but usually sells out its Tuesday "Wing Night."

In Fulford, Raven's Nest, next to the ferry parking lot, offers great omelettes and is especially popular in the mornings for its coffee, cheese scones, and cinnamon buns. Ethnic cuisine in Ganges includes Chinese, Thai, European, and Greek. Steve and Georgia Asproloupos are delightful hosts at their Bouzouki locale on the Grace Point waterfront. Next door is Alfrescos, offering a variety of specialties. Nearby at water's edge, Sea Court features chicken and steak. House Piccolo is a fine Scandinavian restaurant in a quaint converted home on Hereford Avenue in Ganges. Many locals rank it their favourite. The well-named Dares to Be Different offers vegetarian dishes.

Fun places with good value include Maxine's Boardwalk and the Salt Spring Roasting Company. There are also three good bakeries, Embe's, Barb's Buns, and Sweet Arts.

Those in search of the finest in dining may want to splurge at Hastings House, the world-renowned inn that caters to jet setters with deep pockets. Running against the grain of the island's "gumboot casual" attire, the formal dining room at Hastings House offers a set-price, five-course menu nightly and a famous Sunday brunch. Men must wear dinner jackets in this room. The Snug, next to the wine cellar,

This Southey Point farm boasts a setting hard to grow tired of on Salt Spring.

is a little more casual with a four-course meal. The most novel feature is the big kitchen table where guests can simply hunker down to a fabulous repast with the chef in his kitchen.

A COMMON DENOMINATOR

If there is one characteristic that either attracts people to the island or has an immediate impact once they settle here, it is nature. An unusually high number of people have embraced the concept of an interrelated planetary ecosystem and have become conservationists, naturalists, and environmentalists as well as just plain enthusiastic gardeners.

The Salt Spring Stream and Salmon Enhancement Society works to restore and protect creeks on the island and operates a small hatchery on Cusheon Creek. Members of the Island Natural Growers, a chapter of the Canadian Organic Growers, are dedicated to applying natural organic principles and practices on their farms. They are interested in land protection, land trusting, organic certification, environmental chemicals, and heritage tree preservation.

The Salt Spring Conservancy is a non-profit society that receives, holds, and manages land for the preservation of natural habitats on the island. It assists landowners who wish to learn more about the possibilities of land preservation and the place of land covenants on their land. The Water Preservation Society works to protect and preserve Salt Spring's lakes and freshwater supplies. It supports scientific study and research into water resources and promotes public awareness for water protection. The Waterbird Watch Collective monitors and documents waterbird populations along the coast, lakes, and ponds of Salt Spring and provides data for a variety of national and international scientific studies. Participants receive a field note kit and learn by observing.

A recent addition to the local scene is Jeff Lederman's wildlife rehabilitation centre. A world leader in applying homeopathic remedies to preserve and restore immune systems in young animals, Jeff is developing Island Wildlife Natural Care Centre to service the needs of the Gulf Islands.

The Salt Spring Garden Club encourages local gardeners by sponsoring speakers on all aspects of horticulture. It holds a judged spring show at the United

Church in Ganges, and twice a year (April and October) runs a plant sale at the Farmers' Institute.

Every year in July, the Island Arts Centre Society (Artspring) and the Salt Spring Chamber of Commerce jointly organize a house tour. This is a great way to see local gardens as well as architecture and interior design of many island homes that are otherwise inaccessible. Different homes are on the tour each year. Art, humour, natural food, relaxed lifestyle, a common caring for nature—they all make this a great place to be.

Salt Spring is an island of beautiful small churches, including the much-photographed St. Paul's in Fulford.

5

My Chosen Place

Islander Profiles

SALT SPRING'S POPULACE OFFERS a wonderful blend of humour, artistic vision, seasoned intellect, and homespun philosophy. Any celebration of its past and present must reflect the voice of its people. Pearl Gray has interviewed and completed profiles of fourteen diverse Salt Spring residents.

Geoff Ballard
  scientist and entrepreneur
Robert Bateman
  artist and philosopher
Paul and Anna Burke
  whimsy sculptor and installation artists
Jill Louise Campbell
  artist and gallery owner
Arvid Chalmers
  playwright and humorist
Carol Evans
  self-taught watercolourist
Ute Hagen
  acrylic artist
Linda and Leroy Jensen
  theatre director and artist
Jeff Lederman
  wildlife rehabilitator
Toni Onley
  artist and aviator
Valdy
  folk singer and impresario
Kathy Venter
  sculptor of life-size nudes
Judy Weeden
  "the potter lady"
David Wood
  farmer and purveyor of fine cheeses

GEOFF BALLARD

Shelagh & Geoff Ballard

On Salt Spring you may discover that your newest acquaintances have a history of significant accomplishment in the outside world. Such was the case for me when I mentioned playing tennis with Geoff and Shelagh Ballard. My son Jason asked, "The Geoff Ballard whose company is engineering the hydrogen fuel cell?" A phone call to a friend confirmed that it was indeed the same man. Subsequent conversations and a formal interview revealed both the scientific struggle Geoff's company faces and how home came to be Salt Spring Island.

Ballard's focus on environment-friendly alternative energy sources is based on two negative traits of the combustion engine. It pollutes and uses fuel resources that are being depleted.

Given these drawbacks of the current system, I wonder why he sees it taking as long as forty years before his fuel cell revolutionizes industry. "Ballard Energy already has buses running on its fuel cell in Vancouver and Los Angeles," Geoff explains. "Forty years is the time frame just to get the manufacturing levels up to replacement. Even if you replaced the automobiles at the rate of a million a year, there are 50 million sold every year."

While most laypeople are fascinated by the future of the car, Geoff says "the biggest economy will come in the area of utilities. We'll never again see a rural electrification like we did in the '30s in North America. Instead of stringing wires and connecting a whole grid, we'll see distributive power. You build a 250 kilowatt fuel cell for downtown Ganges. Individual homes would have a 5 or 10 kilowatt cell, or a neighbourhood will be linked with one 250 kilowatt fuel cell most likely powered by natural gas."

According to Geoff, "We have a subsidiary working with General Power Utilities of New Jersey. They're looking at the rural electrification of places like Brazil and China."

I try to sort out the advantages of this for third world economies. Geoff says, "The significance is that natural gas is ubiquitous, it really is everywhere. It is the by-product of decaying organic matter. So you literally can take the city dump and put a big sheet of plastic over it and pipe off the gas. Through a reformer it can power your lights or your TV. You can punch holes down anywhere in the world and get natural gas. The world will phase in natural gas as a fuel …Then oil becomes relegated to the chemical base society and becomes the feedstock for chemical work, which it should."

But will this new hydrogen economy be affordable? "Oh, yes, there is no reason that a hydrogen-based economy can't provide you with the same Btu's or kilowatts for the same price you are paying now for them." And I realize all countries will have more balanced access to energy, instead of the current situation where some have to pay enormous premiums for fuels.

Geoff also details attempts by the oil and automobile industries, to discredit fuel cell technology. He says, "These are people in a privileged position that they don't want to lose." He smiles. "British Columbia was a perfect place to do our research. The mistake that the industry made was just that they ignored us too long." Now there's no way to stop the technology. "The world is well aware that you can have a clean energy economy and we're getting huge support from places like California who just have to have it."

Ballard's company has sold fuel cells to Ford and Daimler Benz so they can experiment with the technology. These are major deals. Ford alone manufactures seven million cars a year, 14 percent of production worldwide. "It won't be long before a Japanese company steps in and once you've locked up a third of the auto industry, the rest of the people have to get in line. The schedule is to have an auto manufacturing plant installing fuel cells by 2001. The thing about technologies whose time has come, like the PC, is that they happen far faster than anybody predicts because everybody gets on the band wagon."

Trying to keep my balance under the sway of this calm, absolutely confident scientist, I ask if he has any competitors? "We will very shortly. A lot of people think they are competitors? but they are still violating our patents as far as we can see." Ballard Energy currently has about 158 patents in its portfolio.

Born in Niagara Falls, Ontario, Geoff graduated in engineering at Queens. He completed a Ph.D. in Geophysics at St. Louis and worked nineteen years in the United States. Salt Spring Island provides a respite from his work. "You can imagine that when you are struggling with an organization that is trying to change how the world thinks, there is considerable stress. [Well I can't really imagine it to be perfectly honest, but I'll try.] You are trying not to make too many mistakes nor give too many handles to your enemies. We found as you got on the ferry to Salt Spring, the burden of the world sort of fell away. We'd come for the weekend, boating, just renewing oneself to go back to the fray Monday morning."

Geoff has been in the fray since 1974. "We didn't jump right into the fuel cell. We thought, like a lot of people, that the battery was the answer for years. Eventually we came to the conclusion that the fundamental physics of the battery was just too tough to make something that would meet 'the mission profile' of the American public. We're very dependent on the automobile in North America and insist upon it being available to us. We're not geared to using up the energy in the car, then plugging it into the wall and not having it again until tomorrow morning. That's just not our lifestyle. Essentially we have to meet the availability of the internal combustion engine where gas in the tank means you turn your key and you can go."

Geoff is a practical man who understands that it is impossible to change human nature. Better to find a technology that meets those needs—and then some. Geoff never doubted the possibility of the fuel cell. The scientific process to make energy from a fuel cell has been known since about 1840. "The science was in place, but not the engineering. We did the engineering. You could build fuel cells but it was very expensive. A million dollars a watt. What we did is we engineered it out of simple materials so it would come in at fifty dollars a kilowatt, which is what it has to be to be commercial...There are three pieces in the fuel cell that you try to bring under control: the amount of platinum that you use as a catalyst. And that seems to be under control...And then the plastics that are used for the membranes are proton-permeable. Then one has to bring down the price of the manufactured parts, like the plates you put together. They also seem to be under control. We can high-volume manufacture all three of these."

And the plants that manufacture pollution-free cars will be run by the same technology. "We're talking about a transformer technology in which we completely replace the energy economy that exists today, with the fuel cell as the conversion device. By 2040 the combustion engine automobile will be moving into museums...A gas pipeline will bring fuel to the fuel cell in your home."

Ballard now has quite a political force behind him. "I don't think any of us anticipated that the whole ecology theme would come on with such immense concern. That really spurred this forward. The green power is being felt by the politicians. It's worth votes." Last year the Canadian government loaned Ballard's company $30 million, a token amount considering the deal with Ford was worth $500 million. "But it was the correct token amount," Geoff says. "It said to places like Ford, the government is behind this. Investment itself is far more important than the amount of the money. It says 'You are part of the society of Canada that the government wants to support and foster.' It would be the same way with B.C. if it chooses to do all its buses to become fuel-cell powered. If you took BC Transit and made a plan to convert all its buses over a ten-year period, it would be significant enough that it would encourage us to put a manufacturing plant in B.C."

But islanders need not worry. Most of the energy that Geoff and Shelagh Ballard bring to Salt Spring in the near future will be worked off playing tennis.

Robert Bateman

Robert Bateman, at home in his studio.

Robert Bateman, one of Canada's best-known artists, moved to Salt Spring in 1985 with wife Birgit and the two youngest of his five children. A Toronto-based high-school teacher for twenty years, Bateman chose the Gulf Islands as home for two reasons. They assured his proximity to nature and buffered his family from the urban preoccupation with consumerism.

Bateman's life is a love affair with the planet Earth. "I can't conceive of anything being more varied or rich," he says. "Its crowning beauty is the natural world. I want to observe it and to understand it as well as I can."

A man of many dimensions, Bateman's choice of Salt Spring as a permanent home is by no means insignificant. Bateman first travelled around the world by Landrover in the late 1950s and taught school in Africa in the mid-1960s. Even then he was an active naturalist and conservationist. In the '70s his powerful style as a painter won him a following that permitted new freedoms and the ability to pursue his dreams full time.

Ironically, Bateman sees freedom as a double-edged blade, cutting both ways in our society. His social conscience has spurred him to speak out on many issues including crime. The North American "worship of freedom at all cost" has resulted in "a celebration of disrespect and the encouragement of rootlessness." Bateman observes that in most of the continent, "we no longer have connections to a place and its people." Salt Spring, it seems, defies the norm. Here people, even some who on the surface may appear rootless, do embrace both place and their humanity.

A strong advocate of revised thinking on crime, Robert Bateman applauds some of the traits he found on Salt Spring over a decade ago. He says, "Salt Spring is one place where home-grown values have fended off the material seductions of commercial television." In a paper on this subject, Batemen states, "We have pressures from two directions working on our youth...we train them to be self-indulgent, to worship consumer products...on the other hand, any job [they get] will likely be temporary."

Bateman has come to appreciate the collective commitment to slow growth and controlled development under the aegis of the Islands Trust. It is a rare government perspective that he values. "Generally speaking, we've let our technology get ahead of our conscience," he tells me. "Unlimited growth is not natural."

Although comfortably ensconced in a beautiful water-front home, Robert Bateman is a citizen of the world both in terms of his audience and his interests. His original works are housed in many museums and a recent exhibit drew record-breaking crowds to Washington's Smithsonian Institute. Honorary doctorates, the Order of Canada, and schools named in his honour are but a few of the accolades he has received. Yet he remains humble before all that is natural.

Influences in Bateman's life run from impressionists to economists and demonstrate a basic pragmatism. His "giants" of art include Winslow Homer, John Sargent, and the Spanish artist Joaquin Sorolla. "Sargent just knew how to lay down paint. I sort of do," he reflects, at ease with his own limitations. Bateman was himself "laying down paint" during much of our conversation. He does use photographs to support the creation of his paintings and is certain that most wildlife painters share that habit. If North Americans tell him his work looks like a photo, he accepts it as a compliment. "The same comment from a European would be meant as an insult," he says. Ultimately his talent lies in "capturing the essence of a fleeting moment. I'm after that. My heroes are the ones who can say a thousand blades of grass with ten brushstrokes instead of a thousand brushstrokes. It may look like a photograph, but it is just an impression."

Robert Bateman applauds another hero regularly as he deplores the quest for a global economy. This is E.F. Schumacher, author of *Small is Beautiful.* Salt Spring's artist/philosopher quotes Schumacher regularly in lectures and letter-writing campaigns that condemn excessive consumerism and youth as a "target market." While many Salt Spring residents may share his philosophy, it is unlikely many can match his commitment to his work. His painting comes from an abiding love for the diversity of nature, but the work also serves as a vehicle of awareness. "It's too easy just to look [at Nature]. To have to slave over and capture the quality of the thing, you immerse yourself. That's how [I] can get something out of it."

He is fascinated by the distinct features found within each species of animal. Precise in his observations, he has watched how the fur of a bison may vary both across its girth and from day to day. His time spent in the field has also allowed him to observe human traits. He has developed a special affection for bird-watchers. "Birders don't destroy property. They respect the habitat. They'll come out of the woods with other people's garbage."

After learning of Salt Spring from some naturalist friends, Bateman has called the east shore of Fulford Harbour his home for over a decade. His magnificent wooden house is perched above the clear waters he treasures.

"It's a treat to be able to go out in a canoe, to see water-birds and otters. I like painting water," he says while eyeing the glistening surface. "The way light shimmers on it and reflects off it. As a quick reference, it's right here. I also enjoy the geology...the cliffs are fertile subject matter for my painting."

He, Birgit, and their children walk the wooded trails daily when they are home and participate in island life as his schedule allows. He knows he lives among kindred spirits and has always been a generous contributor to his community. He has donated work to help finance Artspring and participates in any dialogue that explores the values he treasures.

At the end of a lengthy interview, Robert Bateman left one overriding impression. He is a confident, humble, thoughtful man who has found his place to be.

PAUL & ANNA BURKE

Paul and Anna are committed to the environment and their family. They brought their kids to Salt Spring to be on the land, to experience nature daily in a way unavailable to them in their former Vancouver location. They are people who see goodness in all the living things that surround them. I shared tea and conversation with them in their tent house, erected to provide shelter while they build their permanent studio/home. This temporary plastic and can-

Anna & Paul Burke

vas abode was a creative act itself, the floor freshly covered with fir boughs changed weekly by son Oliver; the sylvan atmosphere charmingly enhanced by a large woodstove and many candles.

Paul makes whimsical folk-art sculptures. He captures movement and personality in such a way that it is easy to immediately connect with his creatures. They are playful and accessible. Paul uses found pieces of wood for his works. The numerous holes in one piece of driftwood made it look to Paul like the woolly coat of a sheep. At the hands of the craftsman it became a ewe accompanied by two frolicking lambs. A curved piece of beech wood sat near us, transformed into the graceful body of a cat after Paul added ears, a tail, and legs.

Anna works in many media. For a time in Vancouver she focussed on fabrics and came to specialize in children's clothing. She enjoys sculpturing in clay, but at the time of our interview, wood was her material of choice because the dampness of their temporary home made it difficult to work in clay. When she couldn't find the box of their children's games she had packed away, Anna researched primitive board games and set out to design the requisite pieces and reintro-duce the games. Always sensitive to her audience, Anna soon made a discovery. "To make the games interesting for to-day's children, I had to learn more about the time and culture of the original games. It was often necessary to find ways to enhance the vague and limited strategies of the games." The boards and game pieces took on a dual life. Not only do they serve as playthings, but their beauty allows them to double as wall hangings when not in use. Until the studio is finished, her plan is to sell games with her personally researched instructions at the Saturday Market in Ganges.

Paul explains how they recently came to Salt Spring. "We were both finally working for ourselves in our old house in Vancouver's Chinatown. For many years we had been thinking about leaving the city. We didn't come here because we disliked the city, but what we wanted was a new sense of balance, a connection with land and environment. Our children were pushing for that. They were very much a part of the decision."

Paul looks towards a mixed pile of his cherished chunks of wood. "We looked all over the province," he says. "We spent both sunny and rainy weekends on Salt Spring, and then we found this place."

Paul talks of roaming the surrounding forest and his field outside. The wood he finds on the ground around him is his treasure-trove. "I am always on the lookout for usable shapes and strength. Here I can find fallen branches of juniper wood and never have to cut pieces from a living tree." He smiles, explaining how in cedar roots he sees the manes and tails of horses. He recalls how, when clearing their land, he became "delirious with joy" at finding clumps of cedar roots, as salvaging them elsewhere had always been a time-consuming task.

Sometimes he searches for specific wood. "Arbutus is one of very few woods that branch into three offshoots," so it is "very useful for birds' feet. Not many trees do this and have the strength of arbutus to hold up a figure." He shows me an example as he puts their lifestyle into business-page perspective. "We're quite happy to be doing classic value-added work in the forest sector," he states.

In addition to their smaller pieces, Anna and Paul have gained acclaim as installation artists, conjuring up elaborate images for large-scale exhibitions. Starting with Artropolis, a tri-annual Vancouver event featuring 200 artists, they have collaborated on three shows that allow viewers in the galleries to participate. They developed the idea for the first show when they discovered that their home sat on a former elk habitat. A book on Vancouver's visual history explained that the last thirteen elk in the area had been killed in 1850 only a mile from their home. They decided to commemorate this death with an altar and thirteen 30-inch-high carved elk. "We had no intention to make people feel guilty," Paul explains. "We just set out to make people aware that where this huge city exists was once a wildlife habitat." They encouraged viewers to enter the stage-set-like area and touch the carvings. Anna had recently returned from Japan, and she designed two Shinto prayer trees for the exhibit. The idea was to encourage viewers of the show to prepare and hang their own prayers. The Burkes provided paper, crayons, inks, and carved rubber stamps with images of various animals on them so viewers could be creative with their prayers. "People loved it," Anna recalls. "We could barely keep up with the demand for paper." Over 30,000 people came by during the show's month-long run. "Parents and children participated together," Paul says. "It was the exact opposite of a gallery placing some abstract lump of art in a big room. People loved it."

Such shows are strictly non-commercial art experiences. Based on the success of the Vancouver show, Paul and Anna received Canada Council support to do others. At Victoria's Commonwealth Games they combined a pool of aromatic cedar chips and stylized sculptures of fish in a presentation called "Salmon Spawning." This show travelled to different venues around the province including Nanaimo, Kamloops, and the Queen Charlotte Islands.

Both of them hope to do more. "These shows would become an instant vision in Anna's mind." Paul pauses as if expecting some new vision to burst forth. "Anna is basically an unstoppable river of ideas."

Introducing another example of his wife's artistic range, Paul explains how the Tides Foundation, based in San Francisco, purchased a series of *raku* vases Anna made. On permanent display, the vases featured copper-cobalt glazed images of swimming salmon stamped into the clay. Rain forest tree branches, replete with moss, were placed in the vases. The series evokes a stream and shoreline.

The Tides Foundation sponsors ecological projects, some of which are aimed specifically at wealthy young people, hoping to help them understand their responsibility to the planet—to encourage them to use their financial resources to enhance and restore environments. The Foundation wants to help Anna and Paul take another installation of spawning salmon on the road in the Pacific Northwest.

What have the Burkes discovered since their arrival at their rural home?

Paul thinks for a moment. "Salt Spring Island is a rich community of kindred spirits connected by love and respect for nature no matter what they do for a living. It is conducive to meeting all sorts of people you wouldn't meet in the city."

In recent years their exhibitions have exposed Paul and Anna to many island communities north of Salt Spring. "A lot of like-minded people have come to this area and formed strong artistic pockets—here, Hornby, Cortez, Quadra. I am just coming to realize that together they form a larger community with the same creative and environmental interest," Paul says.

In closing, Paul and Anna confirm that their latest vision is still alive. The sparkle in both their eyes says so. "We wanted space to build a studio. Anna wanted our place surrounded by a field, like Alexander Calder's studio in France." The meadow outside their tent awaited them. It was time to let them get on with their dream.

At the time of our interview, Anna and Paul were unsure when the studio would be complete. To visit and view their latest work call (250) 537-7477.

JILL LOUISE CAMPBELL

Jill was born in Montreal into a traditional family, and although her grandmother painted and young Jill was often a model "dressed in velvet" as she says, she was conditioned to think of art as a cultured lady's pastime, not serious work. "I didn't take it [art] seriously although I knew in my heart it was bigger, but I had to contain it." So in university Jill studied general arts and art history, painting only as a hobby. A year of further study in general arts at the Sorbonne in Paris allowed her to "indulge my lust or love in all the galleries." She devoured anything that she could find on the impressionists.

Jill Louise Campbell with some of her work.

Her return to Canada saw her studying economics at Ryerson, still in pursuit of a "real" career. "But this was the drive I had, to be succcessful. I had to be in a man's world instead of honouring my own truth." After she married, Jill and husband Duart moved to Vancouver where their first child was born. It was at a dinner with a group of business-women who were also mothers where a friend introduced her as an artist for the first time. As Jill says, "These women weren't home full time nurturing children, and she wanted to introduce me as an artist, not as a mother." A new sense of self-identity as an artist took root instantly. It was that moment; it was incredible."

Her first studio was in the bedroom of their tiny cottage, but she got sidetracked again. Duart began to make furniture as a hobby and Jill, in order to be together with him and their two girls in the workshop, began decorating it. These pieces became an instant success and before long the couple was managing a large business. Jill found herself supervising other artists, who copied her designs onto furnishings, rather than spending her days creating her own art. She realized

Scenes of Ganges Harbour may be viewed at Jill's gallery.

she wasn't happy and she knew why. After some introspection they closed up shop, sold their house, and headed for the south of France. With Duart happily in the role of house husband, Jill spent a year roaming the countryside sketching. From France they moved to Salt Spring with a new plan. Duart began to build their dream house by himself, and they mutually agreed that Jill would be the breadwinner with her art.

An idyllic concept at the time, this proved to be a trial by fire for Jill. She painted all week and then travelled around the province on weekends, selling her work. One year she attended over forty home shows. Providing for her family was the incentive to keep going. A few galleries like Northern Passage in Victoria supported her.

With so much work going out, Duart persuaded her to stick to standard formats so they could mat and frame the work efficiently. Jill's next big step was to move her display space out of the house to a more visible location.

Jill's work can now be found year-round at her own gallery on the Ganges waterfront. She shows lively, energetic landscapes inspired by local settings.

She has developed a unique technique in an effort to bring texture to her vibrant mixed-media paintings. In watercolour she works "wet on wet" and draws in gold acrylic to give the work definition and pattern. The gold produces ethereal quality and the result is reminiscent of the work of Canadian artist David Milne.

While the gallery is her show place, her painting is still done in the studio. Ideally, Jill dives into a new piece in a state of pure joy. A confirmed spiritualist, she attempts to paint wholeness. She surrounds herself with her favourite photos, art books, journals, and the music she loves while painting in isolation. Her studio sits on ten acres near Ganges and overlooks the sea and adjacent islands. "I can become completely absorbed. It is a spiritual, supportive atmosphere," she says. Introducing an insight I had never heard elsewhere, she adds, "The Indians never settled permanently here because for them the land had a quality that their dead would benefit from." It is this sense of a sacred place that appeals to her.

As much a good businesswoman as an artist, Jill has worked hard to share her work with a wide audience. She developed a print business to provide moderately priced artwork for a growing clientele. She will paint a custom mat to place around a purchased print, thereby giving the piece an "original" component.

Jill's style and beautiful colours have attracted considerable attention and her paintings are in private collections around the world. Her repertoire includes cottage homes and the animals of this magical island, plus waterscapes captured from her family's sailboat. Together with her family, she now enjoys life with a menagerie of assorted pets and tangled gardens.

Jill is one of a growing number of local artists promoting their work on the Internet. To see samples of her work visit www.jlcgallery.com or discover the Jill Louise Campbell Art Gallery in the Harbour Building, #3 Purvis Lane, SSI, V8K 2S5 or phone (250) 537-1589.

ARVID CHALMERS

Arvid Chalmers

If anybody has shaped Salt Spring's distinct brand of humour in the past decade it is Arvid and his comedy partner Sid Filkow. Co-founders of the Hysterical Society, they and their theatrical troupe have poked fun at just about every institution and political movement in the Gulf Islands since they first discovered their mutual talent.

Born in Scotland, Arvid came to eastern Canada at age nine and took twenty years to make his way to Salt Spring. Like many newcomers who have found the Gulf Islands in recent years, he had made one too many commutes into downtown Toronto. With a built-in affinity for rural life and no desire to see a another city's core, Arvid settled on Salt Spring.

"I had never been to a play until I came to Salt Spring," he recently recalled. On Salt Spring it wasn't long before he found himself watching friends on stage taking part in local productions of plays like *Fiddler on the Roof* and *Jesus Christ, Superstar.* "I just got totally enthralled."

Today, you would never suspect that Arvid Chalmers was a shy forty-year-old with trembling knees when he first went on stage a decade ago. "I had this seven-minute routine about my vasectomy," he says. The scene was a local "amateur hour" for all ages, and as fits his brand of humour, Arvid was geared up to explain the traumas of using his do-it-yourself vasectomy kit. "My daughter had the front row full of ten-year-olds. I guess she had told them that her dad was going to drop his pants. They all ran away screaming when I came on stage." Within minutes the audience was roaring and Arvid was hooked for life.

Arvid is a fountain of one-liners. "Fools rush in, but they usually get the best seats," he offers with the slight trace of a grin. "If you're not living on the edge, you're taking up too much room."

That sums up his philosophy of humour as he and his merry band continue their endless search for satire. Often they just look to the latest edition of the *Driftwood,* Salt Spring's popular community paper. "Take anything and poke fun at it," he says. The Hysterical Society has gained fame or infamy throughout the Gulf Islands and earned a reputation for tackling any subject head on and conjuring a cloud of controversy. Women have their "transition groups," he offers. "In one of our Men's Club skits we have our transmission group where we all sit around and talk about old cars."

Arvid describes a typical brainstorming session of the six regular male players in the Hysterical Society. Basically they sit around throwing out subject matter and relying on their wits. Arvid loves double entendres and the risqué where it fits—or sometimes where it doesn't. He explains their criteria for testing new material. "We run it by Mike's wife, Maggie Hayes. If she thinks it's too close to the edge, it's in. If she doesn't think it's a problem, we don't use it."

Arvid is a realtor by day and a comic by choice. He is a realtor with mixed feelings about development and saves a special jab for sleazy realtors he has met during his career. One of the Hysterical Society's most popular "plays" in recent years was *Paradise Lots,* a real-estate development spoof based loosely on John Milton's epic poem, *Paradise Lost.*

Arvid loves the cultural ambience of Salt Spring. "I feel that for anything you want to do in the arts, there's a venue." He lists an assortment of local sites that encourage the arts. "People here like to laugh at themselves. If you get up and laugh at yourself on stage, it's a natural mix. They come back," he marvels. "They actually pay us to do this stuff."

For some of their early work, Arvid and Sid set up Radio Free Salt Spring near the Saturday Ganges market. "Sid was going to interview one of our better known residents, Jack Webster, who was quite famous then. Webster had a thick Scottish brogue and I was to play his role in the interview." The real Webster [a retired Vancouver talk-show host] showed up in the town square as the show got underway and was soon invited on stage where barbs were hurled back and forth to the amusement of all. As was his wont, Webster got in the parting word. "If I was half as funny as you," he said to Arvid, "I'd slit my throat."

The Hysterical Society now performs on a number of different islands during the summer months. Even though the comedy is based on local issues, it seems to stand up in venues from Victoria to Vancouver. The group of eight just loves to perform. Of the octet, only one had any previous stage experience: 75-year-old May Williamson, who has been with the society from the beginning, worked for the BBC during the 1950s.

Not surprisingly, Arvid relies on both B.C. and federal politics for his monologues. "If you take statistics and the way government feeds them to you, there's always something you can make funny at the end of it."

His observations can be both amusing and cutting. He points to Perrin Beatty, a beleaguered federal government minister who changed portfolios. "When he was the minister of Defence," Arvid states, "he lobbied for an extra ten million dollars so he could buy quieter helicopters. Then they put him in charge of the CBC and he cut two million there so he could silence them too!"

Arvid has a serious side but firmly believes that "the best way to get the story out is to make fun of it." On Salt Spring Island, Arvid and Sid still scour the local scene with their ear to the scuttlebutt. Who knows where the next story may come from?

By his own admission, Arvid Chalmers is amazed how his new comical life came to be. "Sid and I met through our kids on a school camping trip," he says. "One night I watched Sid taking notes beside the fire and I asked him what he was doing.

" 'When I hear something funny, I just like to write it down,' Sid responded.

" 'Well, what did you just write,' I asked? Sid looked at the page and said, 'Arvid, Sheep.' I said, 'What's funny about that?' and he looked at the paper again. 'I don't know,' he finally said." Arvid laughs at this unfinished joke.

No doubt before their comedy days are over, they will come up with the right punch line.

CAROL EVANS

In recent years, Carol Evans' watercolours and limited edition prints have won a wide following. There are currently two books of her art in print and her popularity continues to grow.

Driving up to Carol's studio, I was absorbed by the outcropping of old south-end granite and the colourful hues of lush moss along the drive. She lives what she paints—the beauties of nature throughout the Gulf

Carol Evans working in her studio.

Islands and especially Salt Spring Island, where she makes her home. Her studio, adjacent to her home, features three walls of glass that look out onto the natural forest setting. In the studio, huge logs support a skylight over her worktable.

Carol loves watercolour. After a brief stint of formal training she opted out and is largely self-taught in the medium. Based on a course review at the University of Victoria, she decided she would learn little about actual technique there. After searching for other resources, she settled for solving her own problems. "Now," she says, "I feel that this lack of knowledge has kept my work alive. I approach each new painting with a certain fear—can I pull it off?" Fear, challenge, a sense of accomplishment? She is not fully sure what keeps her going, working day after day with such an incredible intensity that often she must go for long walks just to clear her head. But she loves it.

"Watercolour itself is such an organic medium," she tells me. "It reacts and creates on its own." Carol sees herself as part of a duet, directing her brushes, moving the paint, defining the palette. She has to be ready to respond to whatever is happening on the paper. "Control and letting go—you have to have your reflexes ready for whatever's coming at you—like life.

"The water has an action to it and when I'm working with it, it does its thing. It's unpredictable. There is a certain part that is predictable, but I couldn't tell you how I know." Her own words help her explore her talent. "But I've gotten to know what it will do! I think that's the part I like."

Her eyes roam about the studio, picking up images. "Wherever I look, I did some of it but the water did part of it, too. You can't tell one time from the next exactly what it will do. It feels like nature feels. In a way I'm creating it but it has its free will. That's the beauty of it."

Unlike many people who have gravitated to Salt Spring from urban environments, Carol is here, at least in part, because it is a bigger community than she is used to. Carol painted for five years and lived on Mudge Island, nestled between Gabriola Island and Vancouver Island south of Nanaimo. Mudge had only ten full-time residents, so Salt Spring has provided her with an expanded community of friends and neighbours who she finds "offer incredible support."

Carol works from photographs she's taken, often creating a montage of related images. But short of the general relationship of shapes, she doesn't copy. She adds and subtracts shapes, using the photographs for colour clarification. Currently she is interested in light, how light affects the colour of objects lit by a direct ray of sun. She studies the impact of light as it alters shadows. "When the light hits an object, what was grey and dull will become awesome, it just sings," she exclaims.

Once she has painted a cove or bay, Carol feels she has completed her own form of pre-emption. That special place she has fallen in love with has been claimed by her brushstrokes and becomes hers. And through her original work and the growing list of her limited prints, she can share this new joy with others.

Carol tries to express the passion she develops toward her landscape and the resulting feeling she has for Salt Spring. "When you paint someone's portrait, you feel so tender towards them," she says. "You paint all the little shapes in their faces that have come down through the generations. You become very close to that person. It's the same when you paint a landscape."

The landscape she paints is alive with its own spirit, she says. At one point she made paintings in which she animated rocks, trees, and flowers. This was an easy adaptation because in her early career she illustrated children's books. Carol feels fortunate that what she likes to paint, people like to view and buy. The popularity of her work and the appeal of her subject matter allow her to be an artist who can make a living with her work.

Carol feels a common bond with both the island and its people. "Everyone who lives here has an appreciation of the land." And she doesn't expect to run out of subject matter. "This island has great diversity. Especially along the shoreline, there is a lot of wilderness." She smiles at the thought of her family's new vehicles of discovery. "We just got kayaks. The perspective is low on the water." Images of undiscovered shadows and light dance in her eyes. "I'm getting to places I've never been to before."

Carol's work is locally available through Pegasus Gallery of Canadian Art Seaside at Mouat's Mall, #1-104 Fulford, Ganges Road, Ganges, Salt Spring Island, V8K 2S3, phone (250) 537-2421. Her studio is not open to the public.

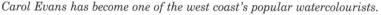

Carol Evans has become one of the west coast's popular watercolourists.

UTE HAGEN

Ute Hagen in her studio with paintbrushes always nearby.

From Ganges, the road to Ute Hagen's studio winds towards the northeast coast of Salt Spring, past Walker Hook in the direction of Fernwood. Two minutes up a narrow gravel lane from Hedger Road, lies the Hagen home and a cluster of outbuildings. Though I am used to the back roads of Salt Spring, the hilltop isolation and serenity of the homestead surprise me. It is February and my visit is blessed by bright sunshine, the first in days.

Ute and her husband, Carsten, live in a restored farmhouse on the eastern half of the old Hiram Whims property, one of the island's original farms. An artist of international repute who paints large canvases in bold acrylics, Ute moved to Salt Spring in 1989. Her charming studio is a rustic structure close to, but independent of the matching house. Inside it feels unconfined, bright, solid— like the paintings that adorn all four walls. It is a workplace that any creative person would covet.

Born in Meissen, near the Elbe River, Ute grew up in post-war Germany and loved painting even as a child. Her talents were natural and she had her first show at age fifteen. A pragmatic father encouraged her to move in less artistic directions. Ute's compromise was enrollment in a craft apprenticeship program. In 1963 she graduated at the top of her class, earning her journeyman diploma, and became Germany's first woman cabinetmaker. She soon immigrated to Canada and worked in the fashion industry in Montreal as a model and later a fabric buyer. She is a woman as vital and sensuous as the colourful, romantic works she produces.

A move to Mexico in 1973 and the convenience of having a maid allowed Ute to begin to paint in earnest. During her decade in Mexico City she painted the human figure. "I was taken by the strong faces of the indigenous people," she says, "especially the women." In their faces she saw both resolve and resignation. In retrospect, she feels they moved her by their stoic acceptance of a life engulfed in paternalism and suffering. Ute speaks of suffering as a requirement to produce good art. "You have to suffer yourself," she says, "in order to come up with something to give to people, something that has emotion."

A few paintings completed during her Mexican years hang on her studio wall. These works emphasize shades of brown and black, possibly reflecting Ute's dismay at the repressed state of her subjects. She also lost her own newborn child during this time, and her palette might reflect personal sorrow. In contrast, the Salt Spring works sing with the colours and vitality of hot, sunny Mexico.

AN ARTIST SPEAKS

I follow the intuition of my soul, painting what speaks to my heart. This way I am true to myself, not trying to please a certain taste in art, but to express what is inside of me—my genuine emotions and human experience.

This ongoing struggle to create a painting that has its own "soul" led me to conclude that it requires more than just the technical and physical, but a deep spiritual involvement. As I enjoy a new challenge with every canvas, I continuously try to express more deeply what I see. My personality becomes the filter through which this expression passes, the work imbued with my own perception and intuitive feelings.

The still life objects, interiors, landscapes, and figures that I paint are all drawn from my everyday surroundings and are a rendition of the quiet and rural life that I presently lead. Truly, I am more concerned that a painting "sings," has movement, feelings, and "life," than that the form is precise or correct.

Ute Hagen

Ute and Carsten returned to Canada, settling on B.C.'s Sunshine Coast in 1983. The monotone greys of a waterfront winter were a shock to Ute's sense of colour. If she had not fully appreciated it in Mexico, here she became aware just how important colour was to her. "I am about colour." She looks at the room around her. Ochres, siennas, ceruleans, and persimmons abound. "Colour helps me through the winter," she smiles. "Winter is bleak. It is not exciting for me in winter."

Her shoreline experience a letdown, Ute and Carsten gravitated inland. They moved to Vancouver, and in 1989, to Salt Spring. In 1991 the Hagens bought the 34-acre Hedger site, and Ute began this phase of her artistic career. Her paintings of recent years suggest that move was a good one.

Ute photographs subject matter to inspire her, to restore her sensitivity to colour—but she paints from memory. At its best, the artistic experience is so intense that she feels she channels her work, that it becomes an expression of the collective unconscious. "I am driven more by colour than subject matter," she says, pointing to still lifes and landscapes that surround her. "I want to transfer the good feeling I derive from them to those who see my work. But," she adds, "the ability to go deep inside to elicit this joy is the result of experiencing much sorrow in life."

This is the first of two paradoxes that influence her work. The second is the nature of the Salt Spring winters— rainy, overcast, and dark. It is in these months of solitude, with Carsten often away on business, that she feels compelled to put colour into life. While she was in Mexico she painted dark; on Salt Spring, her works burst from the canvas like springtime. The paintings fill a personal need and thereby express true emotion. Articulating the process seemed to create new awareness in Ute as we spoke. "I look at photographs until my mind comes up with ideas. I focus on these things. Last year, that whole grey winter, I painted my yellow series."

In the studio she recreates images that summer left behind. In summer she gets too busy tending her garden and managing the twenty acres of pasture and forest that surround her studio. "In summer, it is paradise here." Ute recalls her first visit to Hedger Road. "When I walked onto this land, I was alone. It really felt great. It's like a little Europe. Like Europe in the last century. I saw no evidence of being in the year we are. It's very natural, a very romantic place."

Largely self-taught, Ute's work has been featured in a dozen one-person shows and many group shows. Her clients come from across Europe and North America. In recent years she has participated in group shows in the immediate region, but prefers to sell directly from her studio. Unlike many artists, Ute openly expresses the joy and satisfaction she gains from her work. She likes to have paintings around her. "It is incredible sometimes when people come here, get excited about a new painting, and want to take it home right then." She laughs at the thought of it. "It's hard. Sometimes they are so fresh that I haven't even lived with them."

What has the island given her work? "Peace and nature," she says. "Salt Spring is magic in summer." From her studio she can look out on the fields. She describes the August pasture. "It sings with golden hues." A second large window looks down the descending road that leads from her haven. Ute glances up toward the skylight. "In summer," she says, "the colour of the sky is the most intense cobalt blue, moving to a cerulean toward the horizon."

In the winter months, the studio is her refuge from the grey. "This is an incredible place for me," she admits. "I come into this place and I feel like working. Like translating, expressing, trying again and again. The hours fly by."

In January she draws on the summer memories to develop a new canvas. The apples she picked from her own orchard are transformed with simple brushstrokes into apples more beautiful than I've seen in real life. Ute thinks the real apples are more beautiful and insists that in her work she is only trying to suggest their beauty.

What is her goal? "To express more with less. With a few lines, to know everything is right there." She concludes: "I want these paintings to be felt emotionally. I want to share a good feeling with the onlooker, my fellow souls."

Ute was able to return to Mexico recently for a season of new discovery and a showing of her works at a prestigious gallery beside Lake Chapala in Jalisco province. Alone on this journey, she admits revelling in her own self-determination. She was buoyant with success, joking at her need for an assistant. "Every painter needs a wife," she laughed.

Ute Hagen's Studio is at 180 Hedger Road, SSI, phone (250) 537-4812 or (250) 537-4651.

LINDA & LEROY JENSEN

Leroy and Linda Jensen

The way Linda tells it, "I knocked on this fellow's door, fully intending to give him a piece of my mind. He had done something inappropriate and I was going to let him have it. When the door opened, it wasn't the face I was expecting. Leroy was visiting. A year later we were on our way west to a place I didn't even know existed."

Her story started in a Brooklyn apartment block and the place she ended up was Vancouver, B.C. Linda Jensen's career as a New York actress was cut short by love and an artist who brought her back to his roots in B.C. The year of that trek west was 1967 and they would spend the next fifteen years as city dwellers. Linda had put her career on hold to raise a family and Leroy was a frustrated artist with a day job.

I met Leroy and Linda Jensen at their Salt Spring home, where they have been ensconced since 1982. Although interviewed together, I addressed their careers and current interests individually. Both are fascinating people but a marked contrast in many ways.

Before they met, Leroy was a struggling artist with his share of mental baggage left over from a transient childhood. Aimless for many years, he discovered his passion for art in France in the late 1950s and still has fond memories of the generous ways of that community. Although humble about his own work, there is little doubt that this is where he first discovered his talent. "The best painters were the most generous," he remembers. "They gave their time and a willingness to share their knowledge."

Such was not the case when he brought Linda west, anxious to pursue his work in the closest thing to a home he knew. His memories of Vancouver are not pleasant. Instead of a colony of communal thinkers and willing sharers of knowledge, he found distrust, competitiveness, and politics.

It is safe to say that both Leroy and Linda found an outlet for their creative sides on Salt Spring. While Leroy has found a more acceptable climate in which to paint, Linda rediscovered her interest in theatre and now has her own company.

In 1986, Linda did the choreography for a Salt Spring Players production, *The Wizard of Oz*. She discovered that, "like riding a bicycle, the theatre training was still there."

Her happiness with her chosen home of the past fifteen years is infectious. "I've done things here I never would have been able to do in New York," she says. Aside from doing some writing and forming a theatre company, she has great admiration for the commitment of the amateur thespians she works with. "It is a luxury to be able to live in a community like this, yet be able to do the things that interest you."

Even talking about teaching acting excites her. And it is easy to see why her students respond. "Everyone should be valued," she states. "That should be a given in life, but it's not." She likes working with teenagers and is inspired by the amateur attitude, expecting no pay for their efforts, devoid of ego, willing to give their all to the process of improving. "The process is what I love," she enthuses. "I could work forever toward achieving an end without ever having to *do* the show. Most people need the final reward, but I don't."

Linda sees the local theatre community as offering lots of opportunity and variety for would-be actors. "All the theatre groups on the island work differently," she has decided. "There's no right or wrong but they are all different." Personally, she tries to "help actors develop their role from within." She wants them "to bring their own ideas and energies to the stage."

The magic of live theatre is in her blood. Every night is different and she can talk passionately about the dynamics of the moment when she or her colleagues are on stage. "With every line an actor makes choices," she says. "Whatever they decide to project must be done with clarity if the audience is to respond."

She loves a responsive audience but prepares herself for anything. "There are some times you get in front of an audience and give all you've got and they don't give anything back. They can suck the energy right out of you," she smiles ruefully. "You feel so drained."

Given her own history, what advice would she give to the serious student intent on getting to the Big Apple?

"You need a lot of armour to pursue a career in New York," she replies. "Toughness is as important as talent." She has no regrets about leaving. "I feel very much at home here. I never felt that way in the east, where I grew up."

If actors need toughness, so do painters. Leroy has always sought in Canada the camaraderie he remembers from his days as a student of the arts in Europe. He senses that it could evolve on Salt Spring, but has not found it yet. Not an outgoing man, he admits a willingness to respond to any request for aid from a fellow artist, though he would never presume to offer unsolicited advice.

Leroy has little sympathy for painters unwilling to study their craft, those who simply want to express themselves on canvas without learning the basic principles of technique. Even after forty years of painting, Leroy practises drawing daily. "What would you think of somebody who refused to learn an instrument or to play another person's music because they only wanted to write symphonies?" he asks, suggesting that to gain knowledge of your chosen medium you must expose yourself to others and always be open to knowledge.

For Leroy, Salt Spring is a haven from the modern storm of cultural politics, a setting where he would love to play the role of generous bequeather of knowledge in the tradition of those who shared with him in France.

Feeding off each other, the Jensens have, each in their own way, become an inherent part of Salt Spring's cultural mosaic. They are a resource on which the arts will build.

Leroy's work is available at their home studio on Langley Road. Enter through the framing studio or call (250) 537-4168.

Jeff Lederman

I sense an underlying charisma when I encounter a person who is pursuing a dream. My interest and admiration increase if I conclude that the person's dream is to aid animals and provide shelter for damaged wildlife. Finally, just as I marvel at the homebound salmon, I have to respect anybody willing to swim upstream.

Jeff Lederman with a seal pup.

Such was my reaction to Jeff Lederman when I visited his Island Wildlife Natural Care Centre on a slope above St. Mary Lake. The centre was slowly taking shape in a clearing beneath grey skies. The fruits of a year's labour provided a backdrop to the seal pool where I found him tending one lone pup. While the project is in its infancy, this experienced naturalist has made a unique impression on Salt Spring during his short tenure.

What happens to a dying harbour seal or a wounded deer? Is there any hope for a lead-poisoned bald eagle? On Salt Spring the answer is that if Jeff Lederman and his volunteers hear of it, the animal or bird will be moved to his centre and will quite possibly be saved.

An established artist, Jeff moved to Santa Fe, New Mexico, from Chicago while in his early 30s. He volunteered at a nearby birds of prey sanctuary and was instantly hooked. Aiding golden eagles, great horned owls, and peregrine falcons under the guidance of an avian veterinarian, Jeff found his calling. To broaden his knowledge he moved to a major California wildlife centre that served all species. Next he discovered the Pacific Northwest, drawn to the San Juan Islands.

It was in this serene setting that Jeff became smitten with harbour seals. Ironically, he also found frustration with the Oregon and Washington state wildlife policies of "let nature take its course."

The next stop was the Marine Mammal Center in Sausalito, California, where he worked with sea lions and elephant seals. After a few more stops he decided he was ready to do his own project. Jeff had already decided that his centre had to be near the coast as he wanted to work with seals. Fond memories of the San Juans lingered as he explored the Pacific coast from California north, seeking a home for his wildlife centre. In his search for the perfect setting he discovered Salt Spring.

He was attracted to the island's hospitality. "The people here are friendlier than back in the States." He fell in love with the island, more rugged and treed than the San Juans.

Amusedly, Jeff recalls his entry to Canada from the U.S. Authorities were suspicious of an American's desire to save Canadian wildlife. With immigration, "it took about a month," he muses. "They wanted to know what made [me] think Canada needed Americans taking care of their wildlife. Didn't we have enough problems of our own in the States?"

Lederman's perspective is apolitical. "Animals don't know if they are Canadian or American. The orcas that people here are proud of are the same ones they're proud of in the San Juans."

His conversations with locals convinced him a large number of people here had a naturalist, alternate lifestyle philosophy. This was important because he was determined to include alternative healing modalities in his centre.

The centre is not a zoo and setting it up was not easy. "There's lots of red tape," Jeff says. "We get permits from the federal government. The provincial government issues a wildlife rehabilitation permit." Although there is no vet on staff, one is available locally if required. "I do all the diagnosis myself. I do the treating myself."

What makes the Island Wildlife Natural Care Centre unique is Jeff's dedication to holistic treatments. "Homeopathy, Chinese herbs, acupuncture, rolfing, therapeutic touch," Jeff says. "I do the homeopathy myself and call in specialists as needed." Lederman has working relationships with Reiki and Healing Touch practitioners. He has recently started work with a local associate in efforts to calm animals through natural sedation.

Animal care and comfort is the first priority, so Island Wildlife is not a viewing centre for the public. It says right in the wildlife rehabilitation permit that the animals are not for public display. Jeff agrees with this approach. "Humans stress wild animals. [That can] break down their immune system. Birds can fly into the wall of a cage, doing damage."

During the summer, the seal pools are usually accessible as the pups aren't stressed by people. As well, there is a wonderful video showing, among other things, the treatment administered to a harbour seal. X-rays revealed the orphan seal pup had a damaged spine. The video shows the creature at various stages before he was returned to the wild.

Jeff advises against touching creatures like raccoons or seals as they will readily bite because they are vulnerable. Many could be diseased. "If someone finds an injured or poisoned wild bird or mammal, they should call the centre," Lederman says, "and the animal will be moved by the volunteers."

Jeff hopes the centre will soon incorporate educational lectures and awareness sessions into its program. For now, he has written a beautiful new book that recounts a host of his experiences while trying to save animals. *Cries of the Wild: A Wildlife Rehabilitator's Journal* is both entertaining and educational. The book is widely available and was written by Jeff to help create awareness and raise funds for the centre, which is financed entirely by tax deductible donations.

You can call Jeff at (250) 537-0777 to visit the Island Wildlife Natural Care Centre and view his informative video.

Jeff's book may be purchased at the wildlife rehabilitation centre or from local bookstores.

TONI ONLEY

Toni has been a long-time supporter of the local effort to get Artspring up and running.

How many of us have viewed a misty West Coast mountain vista and exclaimed, "Now that's a Toni Onley"? Toni has captured in his watercolours the very essence of the coast.

Born on the Isle of Man, Toni immigrated to Canada in the 1950s after finishing art school. He started out as a traditional English water-colourist, trying to apply techniques that had been developed in pastoral England to the raw Canadian land-scape. In this hemisphere he was influenced by the abstract expres-sionist movement and the New York School of painting. Later he worked as a minimalist. After a stint in Mexico he moved to B.C., where he became resident artist at the University of Victoria.

It was during this time that he learned to fly. As Toni describes it, "Flying was a substitute for sex" when his wife was uncomfortably pregnant. In any event, flying changed how he viewed the landscape and made places like the Gulf Islands incredibly accessible. He is particularly drawn to Salt Spring because it is a large island with such varied terrain.

Unlike many young Canadian painters today, Toni says, "I have remained faithful to my subject matter." He still relishes depicting mountains and he soars at will amongst his inspirations. Although not resident on Salt Spring, it is only a short flight away from his home in Vancouver and he is here often. Toni's float plane can occasionally be seen taxied onto Chocolate Beach on one of the Three Sisters Islands in Ganges Harbour. Toni likes to paint original works from the same viewpoint, choosing and ordering the elements to suit his current aesthetic sense. He also enjoys painting from the sandy beach on Walker Hook, a secluded beach that

Toni has noted often contains nude bathers. Nudes might be desirable subject matter for some painters, but Toni never paints the figure. He finds it restrictive. "The human form can only be changed so much," he says. Landscape, on the other hand, provides a plethora of shapes from which he can choose. He says he looks at a vista and, unlike a photographer, can eliminate what he doesn't want, use only that part of a mountain he finds interesting, for example, or choose which rocks or clouds he'll include. "I don't paint mountains," he says. "I pick a detail out of a mountain and make my own mountain out of that."

On visits to the islands he often stops at St. Mary Lake before returning to Vancouver. Sometimes he will be inspired by shoreline colours or unique light and take out his easel. He has created many interesting watercolours from the beach at Cottage Resort.

Watching him work is fascinating. He paints with the facility of an Asian watercolourist—fast, with vigour, each stroke making its own statement. "I was very influenced by Chinese and Japanese painting," he says. "Not drawing before I painted; letting things happen on the paper so that in the end it surprises me. Not drawing a line around a thought and then painting it."

Toni jokingly tells people who ask how long it takes him to do a new watercolour, "Oh, about half an hour—and sixty years." Style and technique are critical to individuality.

A fly-by-night artist? Hardly. Pearl always has an eye out for this sky-loving artist who occasionally shows up at her doorstep on St. Mary Lake.

The subject matter is there for everybody. "There is nothing new," he concludes. "All you can do is make your work more personal."

Toni explains he is terribly out of fashion with Canadian galleries "who view beauty with suspicion." And beauty is all he strives for. "Most curators trained in the early '70s look for work with some political message. I treat art and politics as two distinct things." When he paints, he paints beauty. When he has a political agenda, he works through lawyers and parliament to effect change. Toni single-handedly challenged tax law on behalf of Canadian artists, trying to allow them a chance to make a decent living from their work.

Toni has developed an international audience and his work has gained attention and value over the past two decades. Known for donating paintings to worthy causes, he gave a $10,000 painting of Ganges Harbour to the Island Arts Centre Society to help raise funds to complete our local art centre. Prints of that original work are available, for a $35 contribution, at the society office, 7B-121 McPhillips Avenue in Ganges (250) 537-2812. From June 15 to September 15 they are sold at Artcraft in Mahon Hall.

Chain Islands, Ganges Harbour, *1992. Toni Onley donated this painting to the Artspring Building Trust Fund.*

VALDY

For many locals, folk singer Valdy epitomizes the Salt Spring Islander. He is talented, assertive, hard driving, sure of himself. All of this is tempered with compassion, humility, community spirit, and attentiveness to his little piece of the island. He is deeply appreciative of his wife, Kathleen. After sitting with them both I came away feeling I had met real people, just doing their thing and enjoying both their travels and life on Salt Spring.

Valdy spends much of his road time performing at benefits for causes he supports.

Valdy muses over the paradox local comic Arvid Chalmers identified when he noted the impact the singer has had on Salt Spring—that of an anti-developer stimulating growth. Valdy declares, "I'm introduced as Valdy from Salt Spring Island. I'm flagging people to this island, which kind of goes against my grain…Those of us who have a profile are attracting undue attention to the place and thus spurring development on at a rate that is kind of pressing the Islands Trust and pressing the whole other growth cycle." I offer him an out—seeing as it is the business of a performer to attract attention to himself, how could he do otherwise? Valdy slyly suggests that he has his own solution to discourage newcomers. "I tell people it rains from November to April; we get a few bits of sun but most of the time it's wet and grey and many people and relationships have a hard time thriving."

Why do he and Kathleen stay when, like a lot of other islanders, they have seen much of the rest of the world. "On a global basis, I haven't found a place that I personally, on a whole-year basis, like other than here…the socio-economic blend on this island is the most appealing. It is a safe, creative place to be…Culturally it's quite thick and we're on to each other, we have to live with each other. Environmentally, I think people here are striving to be as good as they can to the island. There still are a bunch of island busters, some of them live here, some of them live elsewhere...but the majority of people are looking for a home for themselves and for their families that will be a good place to be."

Valdy is generous with his time and talent, performing at local venues throughout the year. When I suggest that is one of the reasons he is so loved here, he replies, "I like to perform here, but I don't make a living here. It's what I do and people know me as that. And if I were to not exhibit my craft here, people would think I was an elitist, a snob, and I am neither...I like to involve local people with what I'm doing and be supportive of them. When I go on the road it's a different show; it's real show business out there."

Valdy has been on the road for 28 years. Because I've seen them travelling on the ferries together, I ask if Kathleen always goes with him. "Not all the time," she says. "In the beginning I did, naively. But it doesn't make sense, you have to hold down the home fort. And, well, when he's into his own routine, sometimes it means not eating or not going to bed and that doesn't work for me, so I go when it makes sense, when we have friends in a particular area." Valdy's agent in Winnipeg books Canadian dates for him, but, "I'm not home a lot and Kathleen is, so she ends up having to handle a lot of it...but having someone at home who can represent me as well as Kath does is a godsend."

It is Kathleen who tries to explain what would drive a person to be enthusiastically on the road for 28 years. "It's who he is. Valdy will never not perform...it's not a career. I was a high-school teacher. Well, I can be that, do that, move on to something else. It's not true when you're a performer...For Valdy, the performance is a large part of his way of communicating."

Kathleen also keeps him up on local political events, "so he doesn't put his foot in it." Valdy adds, "There is something about Salt Spring that allows people to just be themselves...There is a different attitude when I'm meeting the press in Vancouver or Austin, Texas...The appearance of the life that someone has is as important as what the life actually is...particularly in the American market which is product oriented."

At this point, Kathleen begs to differ. "You don't ditch your persona when you come home. You're very much that persona." And I am inclined to believe her on this one. Valdy does seem to be Valdy through and through. Kathleen observes that Valdy is in fact a contrast to many other islanders in this way, "There are a ton of characters on this island who have made themselves a persona and they play it out here. We have a very theatrical island...The whole of Ganges is a big theatre, look at the Saturday morning market; it's theatre. It's an aspect of Salt Spring that is a very attractive one."

Valdy was born in Ottawa, but his father bought land on Salt Spring in 1941 and another piece, on the other side of Weston Lake, in 1960. Now Valdy and Kathleen live on one piece, just down the road from David Wood's cheese farm, and Valdy's sister lives on the other place. As Kathleen says, "People thought that Valdy moved here because it was a trendy place to live, but he had roots here." Valdy adds, "A lot of people around the world are gravitating to Salt Spring. I don't know what it is about this place, but they say there is an energy on the island that is attracting people. There is a Buddhist enclave up on Mount Tuam, and a lot of spiritual people say they come here because of the energy on the island."

I wondered if this energy influenced Valdy's song-writing. If it does, it is an indirect effect because Valdy does all his writing on the road. "I'm not here enough to get my scene together. I'm constantly juggling paperwork and the tending of the land and the care and feeding of each other. I mean, we have to spend time together. The road is where I have more time...I will go into a room and write furiously for awhile." And write he must because the industry expects him to put out new material all the time. His fans, on the other hand, like to hear all the old tunes. His audiences tend to be in the 35- to 55-year-old range, people who have grown up with his music. Valdy performs to all sizes of crowds but "I like to be able to see people," he says. "The large venues become less personal and thus, in a way, more manipulative from the stage...I like to see the reactions that people are having and work with that." I ask if the audience gives back. "They all do. And if they don't we work very hard until they do. That's essential. If there's not an interchange of energy I'd be exhausted." He continues, "You're only as good as your last gig in this business. Every gig is different and I still get nervous. Well not to the point of extreme anxiety, but yes, I always have an edge before the show."

Valdy's songs address large social issues. "Things that affect humans socially, economically, environmentally...It is a particularly interesting exercise to do something for a specific cause. I just did a gig back in Ottawa, Power Aid, to send money to Quebec for the people who were badly set upon by that ice storm. And we raised a bunch of money. All the hydro workers and other relief workers were seated on the ground floor of the auditorium. They marched them in. Everyone stood and gave them a hand. It brought a tear to my eye. It just felt wonderful, the passion. They had given so much. I wrote a song that day about it. That's when I write the best, when I'm moved by something and there's a crunch on and I have to get it done...And I got 12,000 people singing along. That's wonderful when that happens."

Assisting other performers is another aspect of Valdy's career that is worth mentioning. He and fellow musician Bill Henderson started a Folk Club on Salt Spring. "There were concerts, but there was not a club where people could anticipate that if they spent their fifteen dollars they were going to really get into a performance." They bring in big-name stars like Buffy Sainte-Marie. The performances take place one Monday night a month throughout the winter at Fulford Hall. The shows are not meant to make money, just to break even. I ask how they get big names to come to Salt Spring on a wet Monday night in November? "Monday night is a really bad night for musicians, so it's a bed and it's a couple of bucks. And I do the sound so they know it's going to sound good. At least I hope it is." Valdy produces compact discs for new acts and is proud of the output. "I make sure the artist is comfortable so that they can do their best."

Valdy says he is only good at one thing, music. He has infinite respect for Kathleen, whom he sees as a Renaissance woman with a host of talents. "She's done many things. She's only been sculpting for a year now and she is knocking people's socks off. It's great for me to share my life with her."

I propose to Kathleen that being married to a famous spouse must at times be hard, especially if she is forced to suppress her own intelligence and talent. Kathleen's frank response is what you'd expect from such a woman. "It's hard for me because they [the fans] don't know him. You're supposedly married to this person that everyone knows about, but that isn't who I know. That's not what I know about. We're all human beings. My reality is the guy who knows all the buttons to push." Kathleen understands the performer fascination with façade. "A certain measure of him thrives on the falseness. I find that hard when that balance gets too crazy. And it can. You do feel like the small fish in a big fish bowl at times. I can." She describes her own way of restoring reality. "'Darn it, I just cleaned your toilet again for the umpteenth time, can't you just pick up a brush?' Like a normal wife would say to a normal husband when they get tired of doing something like that. And on some level, I'm sure he is astounded that I would say something like that."

My hat is off to her for being able to stand her ground with such a high energy person. And by this time I can see she has his respect. But maybe it's the nature of folk music itself, its grass-root, communal nature that keeps this man humble even though he is an icon in the business. Recently he did a couple of workshops at the Folk Alliance conference in Memphis. He underscored the fact that in folk music, "we are all individuals and we're not in competition. We are not a threat to each other." He tells me, "The whole audience applauded." Clearly happy with that reaction he concludes, "We were not there to cut each other's throats. We were there to aid and abet each other. And I think it's the same on this island. And with that nature of cooperation, the whole industry can thrive. We look after each other here, and if we pass it around it comes back to us. Community."

KATHY VENTER

Kathy Venter stands amidst her life-size nudes.

Kathy has always sculpted the female nude. The reason is quite basic. "In art school," she says, "there were mostly female models. I learned the language that a female form speaks." And she stuck with it. "If I sculpt a male, the result often feels superficial."

She points out that this is in no way a feminist stance. She simply knows how the female form comes together. "When I started to do the female figure, I started to make sense of who I am," she confesses during our interview.

Much of her work is based on the theme of compassion, a so-called "female" trait that Kathy thinks is largely shunted aside in an aggressive world. Her personal dedication to "resurrecting compassion as an honourable trait" has resulted in her "angels series" of spiritual, compassionate beings that exist between heaven and earth and represent the highest ideals. As Kathy says, "If these angels see wrongdoings, they are drawn into the human fray and take on unheavenly traits. The arm becomes strong and muscular from use. They exude an earthy quality, identical with the terra cotta from which I have formed them—soft, flesh-like, blood-coloured. Their whole raison d'être is compassion and the kind of love that has no holds barred, an unconditional love." Her brow furrows in dismay as she continues. "The world, by and large, sees these qualities as weaknesses, yet they are the divine."

An intense, passionate South African, Kathy's was one of a few white families that lived in the black homelands during her youth. She watched enormous political oppression of their black neighbours who were her friends. As a consequence, she grew up feeling no freedom herself.

When she first came to Canada, Kathy was overwhelmed by both the lack of suppression and the liberty afforded everyone. It wasn't long before her new sense of freedom was reflected in her work. Whereas she had been sculpting very centred, balanced works in South Africa—reflecting a need, she thinks, to contain and protect—she celebrated her new sense of freedom by creating very baroque works. After her arrival on Salt Spring, her work started to take another turn.

Kathy finds the environment here protective and the models open. She suspects that more people are willing to be models here than in other places she has lived because of this sense of ease. The model is very important to Kathy. "Sensuality is wrapped up tightly into confidence and self-assurance in the figure," she says. "It doesn't have so much to do with how she's made as who she is. I get that from the model."

The island, too, has affected her work. "Salt Spring is a place with physical space that creates psychological space," she has decided. Her work has shifted from using the model to give her a way to sculpt her idea, to letting the model speak through her. Not interested in projecting the dark, shadowy side of life (although she recognizes only too clearly its existence), Kathy intuitively seeks out models whose humanity is something she wishes to express.

Her favoured works are life-size nudes. She explains, "Life-size speaks to people; they can relate one on one. Smaller works become objects, something the viewers can remove themselves from psychologically. Life-size makes the statement more accessible."

The sculptures are hollow, Kathy points out. This means that the sculptor forms the body as an encasement, a wall enclosing a void. This sense allows her "to feel the volume of the model—its three-dimensionality."

Most important, though, is the extent to which she strives to render a complete personality or psyche. Where, historically, male sculptors have focussed on the superficial aspects of female sexuality, the breasts and pubic area that are the most immediately pleasure producing, Kathy wants the viewer to see the more subtle aspects of female sensuousness. "The hands and feet, a head dropped to the knees of a sitting figure, all express the deeper qualities of humanity, which is what really makes someone sensuous," Kathy says.

Is this, then, the role of the female artist today—a voice to help women explain who we are to ourselves? Can she restore a respect for those qualities of our humanity that many of us have ignored in favour of narcissism?

Kathy's figures speak with a quiet, self-assured confience. I stood eye to eye with one such female form in her Grace Point studio as Kathy spoke.

"When you look at that figure, that is a cool, composed woman. She is at home in that body. There is not conflict between the psyche and the body. There is not a sense of evil, arrogance. There is not flaunting."

Kathy's works are so human they need to be placed in the soft, human environment of our homes. How alone and vulnerable they would seem in a granite and glass museum. See her work in her studio, Vortex Gallery, Grace Point Square, 1102-115 Fulford-Ganges Road, Ganges, Salt Spring Island, (250) 537-4749 and imagine it in your living room.

JUDY WEEDEN

She arrived on Salt Spring at the beginning of the 1990s after twenty years as "the potter lady" in an isolated Alaska community. There she worked in a converted garage with an outdoor kiln. She laughs, thinking back to some of her northern experiences.

"I remember one day after I had loaded my kiln. It wasn't that cold when I started, but the temperature kept dropping. It was outside and the kiln just wouldn't fire. The next day I wrote a note to myself not to fire

"People seem to want art pieces they can display, functional things." Judy Weeden feels trends are changing.

when it was twenty below Fahrenheit!" Judy's eyes scan her grand studio. "Here, I can fire anytime."

We are sitting in a converted pig barn on northern Salt Spring. In the distance, across a sea of hayfield, the only visible building is Ute Hagen's studio. The two homes share the original Whims farm, settled by a pioneering black family in the mid-nineteenth century. Judy points to a row of trees outside her window, explaining that Mrs. Whims had planted them just before she died. "I just love it. I spend endless hours out here."

She believes that work space is critical to the quality of her work. "I need to have adequate space to work in." Otherwise, she fears, "the work is going to look cramped and uptight."

Judy currently ranks as one of Salt Spring's foremost potters. While her work has a functional aspect, the emphasis on her carved designs gives it a distinct artistic quality. Among her major influences she lists the geometric ingenuity of M.C.Escher and the patterns favoured by southwest Indian art she has seen in New Mexico and Arizona.

Judy leads me to a pot she is currently working on. "I

carve when the clay is hard," she says. "That's what I like to do, so that's what I do. I like to work free-hand. A straight edge can make the work look manufactured." The intricate designs can take four to six hours for a single pot.

Since coming to Salt Spring with her husband Bob, Judy has focussed on creating geometric designs, which are in high demand. "Before I came here, I was all over the map," she says. "Where I was before, there was very little competition. It doesn't work that way here. We must rely on people taking our work off the island."

She estimates that the local demand for her work became saturated after about three years. Now Judy sells her work through two Vancouver galleries and the Off The Waterfront Gallery in Ganges. That and the work she displays in her own studio gallery is all she can produce. An eastern Canadian gallery has asked for her work, but she cannot fill the demand.

Both Judy and Bob, a retired professor, work full-time. Bob grows organic vegetables and is chair of the Island Arts Centre Society. Judy describes her schedule: "I make pieces about three weeks a month and do the glazing and firing for one week. Firing is the most expensive part. The kiln doesn't fire right unless it is full anyway. It takes me about four hours to load the kiln, it fires for half a day and then cools."

Like many potters, she has her favourite glazes. "I know the glazes that work for me. They go with my pieces."

Although she pots year-round, "summer is the crazy time," she says. She has opted not to be on the studio tour map, although her studio is open to those who seek her out. "People who buy my pots have seen them in Vancouver or at the Waterfront. They know my work before they get here and they know the price range."

Her work is not inexpensive, nor should it be. She can spend a day designing and carving a single piece. Also, the perils of the process mean that work that has consumed hours can fragment while being fired. Her studio has a few such relics in the corner.

Two Salt Spring events currently spark her enthusiasm. After sitting out one year she has decided that the spring's Erotic Art Show has really brought the island's artists together. She has a piece ready to display and applauds the quality of work she saw at last year's show. Judy expresses ambivalence about juried shows. Ultimately she expects that the very growth of the Salt Spring art community will lead to exhibitions like the erotic show having a "juried" component.

Aside from supplying her galleries, Judy's personal energies are largely reserved for a September event called "Through the Fire." This has become an annual six-person show organized by herself and five other esteemed Salt Spring Island potters—Terry Ryals, Gary Chernoff, Denys James, Melissa Searcy, and Susan Hirst. The event is held in and around the Weeden studio in a magnificent autumn equinox setting. Complete with demonstrations and work especially created for this exhibition, the event grows annually.

After 25 years at the potter's wheel, Judy admits she's slowing down a bit, but so is the demand for some pottery. "The craft scene is changing," she observes. "People aren't buying coffee mugs like they used to. People seem to want art pieces they can display, functional things. Mind you, I don't think many actually use them, but they want pieces that are accessible, understandable, and there must be at least a hint of function about it."

What does Judy Weeden see for the future of her island? "In my mind it is the growth of the art community that will make this island. There is some very serious work going on here. You feel you are in an art community. That is important."

With that she bids me adieu and turns back to what is important—her work. On Salt Spring you may visit the Weeden Studio, 125 Primrose Lane, (250) 537-5403, or the Off the Waterfront Gallery, 107 Purvis Lane, Ganges, (250) 537-4525.

DAVID WOOD

David Wood with his sheep.

Driving up to David Wood's home and traditional cheese farm, I find that early spring has left a gauntlet of large, water-filled potholes on the winding entry lane. This is a sharp contrast to the sparkling clean workroom where I find David finishing up his morning chores. He leads me across the covered breeze-way and we settle at his large country kitchen table. Everything about David and this room suggests a man of success. I can't help but wonder aloud how he explains his ability to achieve positive results in whatever new enterprise he takes on. After all, a Salt Spring farmhouse is a long way from the specialty deli and catering business that won him fame in Toronto.

David answers quickly, "Well, it depends how you define success. If you're talking about making a lot of money, we haven't been successful yet at anything, whether Toronto or here. The business in Toronto was successful in the sense that it was recognized by a lot of people as a good operation. The same applies to the cheese operation here. We've been working up to it for six years, but we've only been selling for a year and a half. It's certainly not financially successful at this point, but I'm still confident it can be, at least to the extent that it can provide a living for a family." He pauses, then adds, "Although I don't expect it ever to be a cash cow. With farming, if it can provide a living, that's successful. Where Salt Spring is concerned, we want to have enough money to live here comfortably. Those are our definitions of success."

It's an honest answer, especially from someone who has articles about himself appearing continuously in Vancouver publications that are interested in quality food products and experiences. What I am really trying to ask, though, is given that some people have trouble figuring out how to be famous once, how does he explain his seeming ability to become famous with whatever he touches?

"Oh, that's different," he exclaims. "We got onto the right thing at the right time. You know, in Toronto, we started a gourmet food operation at the beginning of the greedy '80s when everybody was ready for such a thing. It wasn't an original idea. Those kind of operations exist in New York, certainly, and all over Europe. If the cheese thing becomes well known, it will be for exactly the same reasons. You know, making cheese on a farm isn't exactly a new idea...It's relatively new to North America, at least the revival is new. Small-based cheese operations died in the '50s, mostly because of consolidation in the dairy industry. You just couldn't survive as a small-scale producer."

That all seemed logical, but I muse, if all those others couldn't make it, how does David plan to survive? David shows his up-town savvy by responding, "Because there is a segment of the market that is educated, well-travelled, knows about specialty cheeses because of going to Europe and the rest of it. They have the money to indulge their tastes. To be knowledgeable about food and wine is a good thing. It is also a good thing to be interested in local stuff, local products. It's a very great trend in North America. So taking all these things together, it's an ideal opportunity for a producer to find a product that fits those criteria. And wine clearly was the boom one in the '70s and '80s and to some extent the '90s. It seemed to me cheese was one that was sort of coming along, and when we moved here eight years ago, it certainly hadn't appeared in Canada yet. There were two or three cheesemakers in California and a few in New England. It seemed like an opportunity."

David lets me in on a more open, nourishing side of himself as he continues, "That wasn't why we came to Salt Spring. The plan came after. We came to Salt Spring because we wanted a saner life and more of a family life. The intention was just to come. It was not really a courageous act but one of almost desperation, really, realizing that if I just carried on in the city it would be a classic situation that if you kept going your kids would be grown up and you'd wonder where the time went to. Our kids were four or five at the time. I was working like everyone else does in the city, I was working a hundred hours a week. Ideally I was looking for a way of life where home and work was not separated and the farm is a natural thing for that." And how did he handle the change from bustling Toronto to Salt Spring? "It felt like a tremendous relief," David concedes. "It's not just the pace of life, it's the tension. Especially when you're running a small business. Life here seemed to be very unpressured. But there was a tremendous amount of stuff to do, fences to build, shelter, all the bits and pieces. Although no money was coming in, it was a lot of work....

I was still puzzled about how he expected to make a living as a cheese prodcucer when farmers all over North America, all over the world, are complaining about not being able to make a living with farming. "I produce a product that you process in some way and add a lot of value to, an agricultural commodity, you have to give it a brand name somehow. And Salt Spring Island Cheese seemed to fit the bill. And sheep seemed to be a natural fit on Salt Spring."

As David continues, I see the mind of a problem-solver at work, making it up as he goes along. "We mainly use sheep. Sheep are seasonal milkers, only about seven months of the year. So the rest of the time you either buy milk or you don't do anything. But we couldn't afford to do nothing, so we decided to buy milk. Hopefully, as time goes by, we'll develop a range of products based on mainly sheep's milk but also goat's milk and cow's milk. Goat's and cow's milk wasn't part of the plan; it's a financial necessity. You can't get enough sheep to keep us going. The problem is the quality. No one has tried to milk a sheep in North America so there has been no emphasis on having a good milking sheep."

Fascinated by David's articulate description of the problem, I can only blurt out, "Where *do* they milk them?"

"In Europe, in the Mediterranean. The good milking breeds come from northern Europe, from Holland."

David figured out how to make cheese in his kitchen before learning how to assemble and use his equipment. Apparently it's exactly the same process as used by the large mechanized operations. I am puzzled. If this is so, what makes Salt Spring Island Cheese a specialty cheese? "We're making cheeses that have been traditionally made on small farms in Europe, always in small lots. That's not to say that some are not made in factories in Europe, because they are. But I think people will buy the small-farm made if they can find it. It's a different product. Also, what passes for cheese in North America is cheddar, mozzarella, and Monterey Jack, and that's it. Believe it or not, the majority of cheese produced in North America goes into cheese slices or cheese whiz. What North Americans regard as cheese and what Europeans regard as cheese are two very different things. Fortunately there still is an opportunity for small-scale producers as long as you find the right market. You can never compete if you try to go up against the

David and his assistant show that the art of cheesemaking, even on Salt Spring, relies on both art and science.

big guys, if you try to make a cheddar or if you're just making a commodity."

I ask if his former business experience was a factor in strengthening his ability to position and sell a specialty cheese in such a vast market. "Well maybe. Most of the cheese goes to retail outlets, to stores like we had in Toronto. So I guess understanding retailing does help. Our biggest market is in Vancouver. We sell direct. It doesn't seem worthwhile to have a distributor. You have to get the stuff to Vancouver anyway, so if you're going over you may as well drive around to stores and restaurants and drop it off. Then you know exactly what stores and restaurants think about it. Also, we don't produce enough to have to worry about distribution and I doubt very much if we ever will. The key is to try to survive on as little volume as possible…When producing a specialty product, you're not competing with commodity prices. I mean, you can adjust the pricing to make it work rather than thinking you always have to produce more."

That seemed to echo the philosophy of Robert Bateman and other Salt Springers who espouse the adage "Small is beautiful." The personal touch, the producer going around selling his wares, has a certain romance and nostalgia for bygone days attached to it. Surely people were buying a little piece of that idyllic Salt Spring lifestyle in each package of goat's cheese. "Yes," David concurs, "I think that it's part of the appeal…what restaurants like too. They can tell people, yes, it's local stuff. On the menu they don't just call it goat's cheese, but Salt Spring goat's cheese or whatever. Salt Spring Island is a very well-known brand in itself, and if you can attach your name to that…"

I ask this Scot from south of Glasgow in Ayershire how he felt about attaching himself to Salt Spring. He tells me the climate on Salt Spring reminds him of the west of Scotland and the Hebrides where he also spent time. "It's actually a nicer climate here, but it's not that different. Culturally it seemed like a great place to be because everybody else was here for more or less the same reasons. There was no major culture shock here. I found the place remarkably open to newcomers. Even the old timers. I mean, Mike Byron, he was very helpful from day one. And he and that crowd have more reason to resent people like me than anybody. We messed up their island royally. But I guess there is such an overwhelming majority of newcomers."

Yes, I thought as I wound my way home, there are a lot of newcomers and most have a story to tell. I'd contemplate that after I picked up some of David's cheese in one of the food stores in Ganges on my way home. Salt Spring Island Cheese is available at most food retailers and the Saturday Market.

Tracy Stibbards takes a stroll through the Saturday Market.

MEMORIES ARE MADE ON SALT SPRING ISLAND

The sand castle competition is a popular event during the annual Sea Capers festival held in mid-June at Drummond Park, Fulford Harbour.

Hailey and Hayden on the beach of Fulford Harbour. Fun in the sun!

A tribute to Mom and Dad. In May 1997, Suzanne, daughter of Gladys (Patterson) Campbell, returned to Salt Spring from Vancouver to marry Paul Hartwig in the same St. Mary's church where her parents had married 30 years earlier. The Patterson family has run the Fulford General Store for generations.

SCENES TO SAVOUR

1. *Back road charm is yours to discover.*
2. *Beaver Point road acreage.*
3. *Seals in the inner harbour.*
4. *Rainbow over Ganges Harbour from Salt Spring Way.*
5. *Sister Islands from a hilltop vista.*
6. *Inquisitive sheep.*
7. *Long Harbour statue.*
8. *Vesuvius Bay ferry terminal.*

5

6

7

8

Gulf Islands Driftwood

Ninth Year, No. 8   GANGES, British Columbia   Thursday, February 22, 1968 $3 per year. Copy 10¢

MILK RUN FROM FULFORD HARBOUR

Kevin Luten swings a can at Roger Hughes.

FISH ARE ESCAPING

✶ ✶ ✶

AND THEY ARE BIG FISH

Fish are escaping from Weston Lake. And they are big fish, at that!

Gavin Reynolds told Salt Spring Island Rod and Gun Club that he took a 7 1/2 pound trout from the Beaver Point Lake last week and weighed it in at Mouat's to prove his point.

There are plenty of fish bigger than that, he told M...

The fish are being down the creek at th of the lake and ther there because they back to the lake a live in the creek b

There has been the outlet for man ported Mr. Reynol guard the fish. T deteriorated and t barrier to fish bein through the outlet.

The club approv ement of the scre

IT'S EARLY FOR GEESE

It's early for geese, particularly Canada geese.

Doug Wilson, genial ship's officer on the Vesuvius-Crofton ferry, was surprised to see a flock of Canada geese fly past a week ago.

He couldn't be sure whether they were a group of 1968 geese heading north early or a flock of 1967 geese which had mistaken Salt Spring Island for Florida, and had elected to winter here.

NIMRODS PROTEST FERRY

SPEAK JUST IN T

Salt Spring Rod and Gun Club got into the ferry picture just in time.

On Thursday evening members endorsed the plea of Salt Spring Chamber of Commerce for the return of the late Friday evening ferry from Fulford.

Gavin Reynolds reported that he understood that the service had been re-established late last week and that the Friday sailing would be maintained during the summer months instead of the Sunday service.

Earlier in the yea Authority had aske of Commerce for it the directors of the asked that the Frid sailing be retained service was to be su

The sportsmen's through under the v following morning ferry service at all had been suspended settlement of the d cut-backs in sailing

10th ANNUAL RACES ON T

Next week is the 10th birthday of the annual pancake races at Ganges.

feasting at the com of Lent.

Small change...

CUT OFF! ● STRICKEN!

GULF ISLANDS ARE HARDEST HIT AS ALL SERVICES STOP

Only real separatists in Canada this week are the people of the Gulf Islands cut off from the rest of Canada by the ferry strike.

Problems of supplies and costs are already being faced by islanders.

Provincial ferries came to a standstill on Friday and for one day the only ferry operating in the vast provincial fleet was the Vesuvius Queen. By Saturday even the small Crofton ferry had been withdrawn from service and the islands came to a halt.

Capt. George Maude, veteran island ferry skipper, recalled this week that the Fulford-Swartz Bay link has never previously been broken for so long a period. When only the Cy Peck linked Salt Spring Island with the outside world it was never off the run for more than two days at a time, even for overhauls.

Service was suspended when

NO FERRIES

ority of islanders were grounded.

Hopes that the strike would be rapidly settled and that the islands would be rescued proved futile. On Monday the striking crew members announced that they would defy orders to return to work.

The following morning saw split into two camps.

On one side were those who thoroughly sympathized with the striking ferrymen. They were mildly at odds with those who contended that the strike was improper and unreasonable.

In the meantime islanders

Strike Dijest

Ferry strike brought problems in its wake. It also brought some surprising incidents.

One Salt Spring Island woman thoroughly sympathetic with the strike, refused to use the still operating Vesuvius-Crofton service. She chartered a fish boat and made the journey across the water in the small vessel rather than patronize a vessel which was not observing the strike.

Mike Stacey brought out his big charter boat to bring students from the outer islands to Ganges for school on Monday.

Group of teachers and others engaged in the Cowichan Valley chartered a fish boat to make a regular morning trip across the water.

Members of the SeaBee Club from Vancouver could afford to ignore the strike on Saturday when they flew into Ganges, high above the strikebound ferries.

Mrs. Warren Hastings was indignant on Tuesday when the re-

The Gulf Islands Driftwood *community newspaper is an institution on Salt Spring. It has been owned by the Richards family for over thirty years and is now reputedly the largest independent weekly in British Columbia. The Peter Lynde caricature captures the jack-off-all-trades persona needed to be a successful independent publisher.*

6

THE GULF ISLANDS DRIFTWOOD

Alice and Tony Richards

Book designer and former Salt Spring social butterfly Cathy Mack at one time worked as production manager for the Gulf Islands Driftwood—*the historic newspaper of record for Salt Spring and its neighbouring Gulf Islands. Here she interviews publisher Tony Richards about all the changes down through the years.*

CM: When did the paper start?
TR: A long time ago. The first owner must have run it for four or five years, then he sold it to Jim and Eileen Ward—he was a teacher and she had experience as a publisher. They sold it in 1966, late '66, to my Mom and Dad [Frank and Margaret Richards]. By the time they bought it, it was being printed offset.

CM: Oh yes, I remember seeing the old paper. You'd be reading a front-page article and all of a sudden, mid-story, it would end with a...*to be continued next week*...
TR: [laughs] We had two electric typewriters. One did 8-point type, serif, Times Roman, and the other did 10-point sans serif, and the headlines would be set one letter at a time. You'd put the letter inside a slot, flash the light on and

expose the letter onto photographic paper, and once you had about four or five feet of letters you'd go into the darkroom with it, cut the paper off, put it in the developer, fix it, dry it, wax it, and cut it up. Every headline was set one letter at a time.

CM: Imagine trying to do that now! That is hilarious!
TR: So most of the headlines in the paper—story headlines, display type, and ads—were set in 10-point type.

CM: Did your parents live here then?
TR: No. Dad was the editor of the *Sidney Review*. He was there for a number of years. Then this paper came up for sale and they decided to buy it.

CM: Did you work in the paper as a kid?
TR: I started at the *Sidney Review* when I was fourteen, and then the whole family worked here when my Dad bought this paper. We took turns doing different jobs: taking pictures, typesetting, answering the phone...

CM: And then you left the island?
TR: Yes, we [Tony and his wife Alice] went to Reid Island, but we grew tired of being broke all the time so we moved back. We worked here at the paper for a while. Alice did the production. I was a reporter. After a couple of years, Alice and I decided we wanted to stay and be more involved in the newspaper. In 1979 we took over the operation from my Dad, Frank.

CM: How has circulation grown over the years?
TR: With the population. The circulation now is 4400; in 1967 it was around 1500. In the early days we covered the outer islands—there were outer island correspondents. Then we started the *Island Times* in '86/87 and we converted all our subscriptions from the *Driftwood* to the *Times*. But we were put out of business—I don't really want to get into that one again—and as a result we lost a lot of money and never really regained our outer island subscribers. But we still cover some outer island news: the Islands Trust, the school district, the CRD [Capital Regional District]—we're all part of it.

CM: What's the biggest story the paper ever broke?

TR: No one big story stands out because this isn't a suburban paper. As far as major newsbreaking stories, that doesn't apply here. We're more feature oriented. But lately, in the last couple of years, we've seen more crime, more sexual crime, more violent crime. Not a lot of it, but when those things happen we have a different kind of news story on the front page.

CM: What about the retreat on Mount Tuam? I remember when the Buddhists emerged after three years, three months, and three days—and a reporter had to hustle up the mountain to get the first shot of them.

TR: [laughs] I heard a rumour that one of them made directly for the Fulford Inn. But of course that was never confirmed.

CM: Has the paper's editorial stance changed?

TR: The paper's stance is basically pro-island—looking for the best for the island. We look at any issue and we consider what's the best stance to take, what's going to benefit the island most. That's our stance on all issues. For the last two years now, a group of us will meet on a Monday afternoon: all the editorial staff, the publisher, anyone else from the staff who wants to attend, a member of the public, and our cartoonist. We sit down for 45 minutes and the agenda is to discuss the topics for the editorial, what our position is. And then we talk about the cartoon, feed the cartoonist ideas, and he comes back the next day with his cartoon. Generally it's me who goes to the meeting with the editorial ideas—one or two topics. I'll say: "I'd like to focus on this topic; here's my take on this." We don't take a vote or take issue, it's just a way of getting ideas, having a sounding board. Instead of writing an editorial from our own personal take on an issue, we get to share it with some other people first, to encourage editorial writers to hear other people's views on topics. It's a healthy discussion and we've won a few editorial awards in the last few years too, so I think it has helped.

CM: I've just read the latest issue, namely the Letters to the Editor: "You've got it all wrong. *The Driftwood*...They always get it all wrong!"

TR: [laughs. He's heard it all before.] Yeah. The word of the week this week is: "Shame on you."

CM: Embarrassing and proudest moments?

TR: Well, let's get rid of the embarrassing one first. There's only one that comes to mind—always comes to mind. I'll never forget it. We had computer-typeset classified advertising and occasionally it screwed up. Not often, but this one week it messed up an obituary and instead of the ad reading: "The family and friends of the late Fred Curtis, etc.," it read, "The family and friends ate Fred Curtis." It was one of the most hilarious mistakes the newspaper had made, but the family was not impressed. Fred probably would have laughed like hell. He used to sing: "I like beer, it makes me a jolly good fellow." He would have loved the ad, I'm sure.

Proudest moment—any week when we think we produced a good paper. Three or four times a year out of the 52 we look at a paper and we say: "This was a good one." And then winning awards too. It's always great to come back to the island and write about our awards. Susan Lundy won a Webster Award last year, a fairly prestigious award sponsored by the Jack Webster Foundation. There are a number of categories. Susan won for a series of articles she did on the Mill Farm, a controversial commune on 60 acres of land at the south end that dates back about ten years—a bunch of people tried to set up a community and out of all the fuss and furor the land became a park...They put on a huge banquet at the Four Seasons in Vancouver. Black-tie affair. And the winners are piped in by a piper. They really try to honour the recipients of these awards. I was pretty proud of her.

CM: What's the controversy of the day? What about the never ending Saturday Market saga, should it be allowed to remain in downtown Ganges or not?

TR: Well, that issue surfaces every couple of years. Someone writes a letter to the editor and everyone gets all fired up again.

CM: Your plans for the future. Are you going to stay on?

TR: Well, we've thought a lot about selling, like every other independent paper left in B.C.—there are only about twenty of us now and I think we're the biggest. We've had offers from a few chains, but we've decided not to sell.

CM: What is it about Salt Spring that keeps you here?

TR: I've been here for a long time. I know a lot of people here. We've gone away a couple of times...and of course we have family here, so that has a draw. But what I like most about Salt Spring is the diversity of population. It's attracted people from all walks of life, from all over the world, and it's made for a very interesting mix. [Laughs.]

CM: You can be at any of the local pubs on the island, and at any given time you can be flanked by a millionaire on one side and a sheep farmer on the other. Unless you know them you wouldn't be able to tell the difference.

TR: I think being an island helps create a feeling of oneness, of insularity. It brings people together, it helps, because after nine o'clock you're stuck here with all your neighbours. The sense of community is special. How long can you maintain the sense of community? I think a newspaper plays a significant role in encouraging that sense of community.

CM: What about the avid interest locals take in the content of the *Driftwood* each week? Wednesdays find a lot of people waiting to read the paper, wanting to take issue.

TR: That very diversity of population and interest and backgrounds makes it very challenging for a newspaper. How do you cover all the issues, all the interests? You find yourself catering to a readership that in many ways is better educated than a lot of your staff and who consider themselves to be better writers.

My final question for this handsome island publisher: How have you managed to stay married all these years on Salt Spring?

TR: Hey, that's a good question! I don't know. There's a lot of people in this office who've been married a long time. I guess you have to come and work at the paper.

7 RECREATION

SALT SPRING AND OUTDOOR RECREATION GO HAND IN HAND. In fact, most people attracted to the island are lured at least in part by the natural amenities, water sports, and West Coast climate. Good information on the variety of recreational offerings, both commercial and free, is available from the Chamber of Commerce or Tourist Information Centre. Also, a wide range of guidebooks on the Gulf Islands give details of recreational activities throughout the region.

Salt Spring residents are aware of many of the facts in this chapter, so it is fair to say that we have included it primarily to help visitors discover and enjoy the natural appeal of the island. Our goal is not to duplicate existing information but to provide readers with a sense of the recreational possibilities on Salt Spring. We want to make sure that visitors are aware of the highlights and we provide extensive detail on some sites based on input from local experts. To supplement our own knowledge we have recruited devotees of various activities who have made Salt Spring their "place to be" mainly because of its great outdoors.

CYCLING

Salt Spring has become something of a cyclist's summer mecca, due in part to its camping grounds and receptive B&Bs. Many visitors forego their cars, riding bikes onto the ferry and spending a couple of days exploring the back roads.

Most experienced pedallers know to apply extra caution on the narrow island roads, but some may not be aware that there are locals who refer to them as "road lice." We haven't had any major problems yet, but there are truckers trying to do their job, and careless bikers who stray too far from the side on a winding road can find themselves in a dangerous situation.

Salt Spring has enough ups and downs to test most bikers. In fact, if you arrive at Vesuvius or Fulford, you are greeted almost immediately by an uphill climb. That is to be expected as most ferries do dock at sea level and that's about as low down as cycling ever gets.

David Payne, author of *Island Cycling*, calls the 55-kilometre Salt Spring circuit the route that inspired his book. He allows two days to tour it all. Off-road cycling is available in both Ruckle and Mount Maxwell Provincial Parks.

In addition to being a great destination for a weekend of outdoor recreation, Salt Spring also offers a base from which to make day trips to other islands, returning to Salt Spring to enjoy the broader choice of food, beverage, and cultural amenities. Mainland and Victoria cyclists who want to ride from Swartz Bay to Nanaimo on a circular tour (connecting back to the Lower Mainland via Departure Bay) can travel from Swartz Bay to Fulford, across Salt Spring to Vesuvius,

Locals and visitors alike enjoy a day of cycling.

and by ferry across Stuart Channel onto Vancouver Island at Crofton. Not only is the route peaceful and picturesque, but it eliminates the steep demands of the Malahat section of the Island Highway. You can rent bicycles in Ganges and Fulford.

KAYAKING

Jack Rosen operates Island Escapades, a kayak service that offers tour packages originating around Salt Spring. Jack has been kayaking the waters off Vancouver Island for over fifteen years and is an outdoor adventurer at heart who loves the opportunities that Salt Spring has to offer. He calls Salt Spring "the gem of the Pacific" and has set up shop on Cusheon Lake in recent years.

"Salt Spring has beautiful freshwater lakes for those wanting a gentle initiation into the sport," Jack says. "It is nice to start kayaking by learning strokes and rescues in St. Mary, Cusheon, or Stowel Lake. Once a student gains confidence, it's off to the ocean to explore."

While Jack's business is strictly guided tours, two other local businesses rent kayaks and give lessons and tours to novice and experienced paddlers. Both Sea Otter Kayaking and Salt Spring Kayaking operate out of Ganges Harbour, while the latter has another "Yak Shak" next to Raven's

Kayak enthusiasts start their adventures from Ganges Harbour.

Nest at the Fulford ferry terminal. For minimum 24-hour rentals, they deliver kayaks to sites around the island, a nice service for those not equipped to transport a kayak.

The appeal of a tour is that a local like Jack Rosen can chart a trip that assures visitors of any skill level a safe and rewarding excursion. Jack loves to take his customers where he can show off the wide array of birds and marine wildlife. Because of heavy boating and seaplane traffic, Jack tends to avoid Ganges Harbour in the summer. "Even so," he says, "it's nice to be able to view blue herons, bald eagles, osprey, and falcons in such an active harbour."

Jack's favourite paddles are to off-island destinations only accessible by watercraft. A fairly easy jaunt from the north end of the island crosses Houston Passage to Wallace Island Marine Park. It is only a mile from two alternate launch points, Southey Point or the Fernwood Wharf. Tent Island, the Secretary Islands, and Kuper Island provide other attractive destinations with lots of birds and seals.

In the south, Jack favours Russell and Portland Islands. On the latter, "a vigorous paddle to Princess Margaret Marine Park" makes for a great outing as long as you stay out of the way of ferry traffic. Jack also likes the less-frequented paddle out of Burgoyne Bay along the west coast. "Challenge yourself to the faster waters of Samsun Narrows," Jack suggests to the more adventuresome.

Prevost Island, accessible from either the Long Harbour ferry terminal or the beach at the end of Churchill Road, now has a B.C. Parks site. This island has long been the pastoral farmland of the DeBurgh family and is an easy crossing from Salt Spring's Nose Point around Selby Point to James Bay on Prevost. Here, the new 235-acre park offers camping and hiking options. Those ambitious enough to circumnavigate Prevost Island had best allow a full day to enjoy the various coves. Groupings of islets at the south end of Prevost offer ideal places to stretch the legs and explore.

North Salt Spring's Great Circle Tour. Kayaking campers launch from the north end of the island to start a fabulous circle tour. This journey meanders across to Wallace Island, through the Secretary Islands, north to Reid Island with its old Japanese herring saltery, then west to where the white-shell beaches of Penelakut Spit mark the entrance to Clam Bay. Kayakers continue through a dredged channel that separates Thetis and Kuper Islands to arrive in charming Telegraph Cove with its two marinas. The return journey to Salt Spring takes paddlers south along the west coast of Kuper to an idyllic sandy cove on Tent Island where a swim, picnic, or overnight camp are attractive options. (Tent Island is part of the Penelakut Band reserve and campers should phone 250-246-2321 to notify the band of their camping plans and obtain permission.)

From Tent Island it is an energetic paddle across Houston Passage back to your launch point at either Fernwood or Southey Point. The best camping options along the route include three sites on Wallace Island, a small marked recreation reserve south of Reid Island, and Tent Island. The entire trek requires about twenty kilometres of paddling.

HIKING

One of the downsides of this island's early settlement is the fact that almost 92 percent of the island is now privately owned. The rest is divided between parkland and Crown land. Finding the best places to hike can require some expert guidance, so it only seemed fitting to talk to Charles Kahn when we turned to hiking. The author of *Hiking in the Gulf Islands* lives on Salt Spring and is an active member of the Salt Spring Trail and Nature Club. Charles' book features thirteen hikes, eighteen shore walks, and fifteen road walks. Naturally, some stand out more than others. With the help of Charles, Jack Rosen, and a few other contributors, we have selected a few of the best hikes and walks on Salt Spring.

Ruckle Park Trails. There are eight kilometres of trails in this provincial park on southeast Salt Spring. The park was originally part of Henry Ruckle's nineteenth-century homestead and the family still operates a family farm on the edge of some of the hiking trails. (Please respect their privacy.)

Maps of the trail system are prominent in the park and show a variety of circle-route options. The full eight-kilometre circuit can be started from the park office (Henry R's old Potato House); a parking lot is nearby. The trail heads north and the full circuit requires a left turn at the first junction. The trail slopes up through forest to a rocky hilltop before descending to meet a second trail. If you stay left and follow this combined trail you will come to King's Cove, once a major log dump, that is close to the site of B.C.'s less-known gold finds.

A ten-minute retreat back down your route will return you to the junction. Turn left and walk past Merganser Pond to another junction. Turning right here takes you back to your parking lot. A turn left takes you to the shoreline section of the Ruckle hike where you will see a panorama of offshore islands. You can follow the trail to a point where a road leads back to your auto or follow the route to Beaver Point and the prettiest part of the hike.

Beaver Point is named after the old Hudson's Bay Company ship SS *Beaver*. The trail passes the walk-in campsite area where you may find a few tents. A navigation light indicates that you will soon be turning inland as the trail cuts past some of Ruckle's original farm buildings back to your starting point.

The Mount Erskine Trail is an invigorating climb through groves of fir, arbutus, and Garry oak. In spring, hikers will also enjoy the flowering manzanita shrubs. After a 45-minute ascent the trail becomes a circuit, so you can go in either direction and end up back here for the return descent. If you decide to go counter-clockwise (i.e. turn right), watch for the turnoff to the lookout twenty minutes after starting this leg of the hike. When you return to the trail after visiting the lookout, make sure you do not take the first junction right as this takes you out of the park opposite to the route home. This hike takes two to three hours.

The Jack Foster Trail at the north end of the island is reached by following aptly named North End Road until you see an intersection with a large fir tree in the middle of the road. Turn on to Southey Point Road here and watch for the red metal trail marker on your right, very close to the intersection. There is limited parking here.

Be cautious at the beginning of the trail: dampness can make things slippery as you drop down to flatter terrain. A fairly level trail bisects mixed woodland for about fifteen minutes before you reach the beach that borders Trincomali Channel. Try to arrive at low tide so you can enjoy a kilometre of lazy beachcombing at any pace you wish. Upon reaching the small breakwater at the far end of the beach, you can either retrace your path along the shoreline or scramble up the embankment for a shorter route back to your car. A short corridor of public land abuts the farm near the breakwater. This connects to North End Road and you can enjoy an easy walk back to your vehicle.

Charles Kahn cautions that some local residents are against further development of this route based on the old

View of B.C. ferry from Ruckle Park.

NIMBY (not in my backyard) mentality. Respect private property rights but be assured that the entire route is on public land.

Other shoreline walks that we rank among the best start at Drummond Park in Fulford, Beddis Beach, the end of Churchill Road, the Walker Hook area, and the Fernwood dock area.

From Drummond Park on Isabella Point Road near the head of Fulford Harbour, or from a second access just about two kilometres further down this road, you gain access to

The Beach House, Ellie's B&B.

the harbour tidelands. At low tide you can saunter at water's edge or splash in knee-deep water to your heart's content. Kids love it here. Also, during crabbing season you will see locals hunting for dinner in the shallows along this stretch. (And the greyish blue home about 600 metres south of Drummond Park is Ellie's Beach House B&B. Wave if you've read this book!)

You might need a keen eye to find it, but Beddis Beach has one unique treat in store—a castle. Before building codes restricted such projects, Winsor Utley, the first president of the Salt Spring Painters Guild, built his castle here. Yes, on Salt Spring, where new construction is limited to two storeys, a five-level, beach-stone-and-cedar abode qualifies as a castle. As you walk north along the beach, this building comes into full view. Coming from Ganges, Beddis Beach is reached via Beddis Road, a pleasant six-kilometre drive in itself. From the south take Cusheon Lake Road, turning right onto Beddis where they intersect. Near the end of the road on the left, a narrow gravel road leads to a small parking lot near the beach entrance.

There is a nice little beach at the end of Churchill Road (out Upper Ganges Road beyond the Harbour House and Hastings House, turn right). Stairs lead down to the shoreline which provides a nice perspective of Ganges Harbour, the Chain Islands, and some of the waterfront homes and shoreline along the Long Harbour peninsula.

Walker Hook is such a nice area that it must be mentioned. However, at this time the public beach featuring Salt Spring's whitest sands is only accessible by boat or with permission to cross private lands. The beach itself is on tidelands, so is by definition public. The surrounding land is owned by the Caldwell family, which has at times posted notices asking people to seek permission to cross rather than trespass. Their interest in maintaining the pristine nature of the area and protecting the bird habitats from abuse is to be admired and respected. They discourage visitors during extremely dry periods also.

Fernwood is a fine beach for intertidal viewing. Jack Rosen says that as a bonus, "You can usually expect a pleasant visit from a local river otter who is as curious with you as you are with him."

Some of the country roads on Salt Spring make for lovely walks in themselves. Beddis Road certainly qualifies, as do the narrow roads out beyond the Long Harbour ferry. Tripp Road on the west side of St. Mary Lake and the roads around Southey Point are also enjoyable.

This is a good place to mention a great recreational map of Salt Spring Island designed by Linda Adams. Called "Salt Spring Out of Doors," the 40- by 54-centimetre map shows trails, beach access, cycling routes, swimming holes and beaches, scuba dives, boat launches, fishing sites, anchorages, government docks, marinas, windsurfing, tent and trailer sites, shellfish zones, picnic and play grounds, golf courses, tennis courts, trail riding, viewpoints, bird-watching venues, berrypicking locales, wildflower meadows, and historic sites.

The map was recently updated and is an ideal supplement to this book, available at bookstores and other local retail outlets.

CAMPING

When the word "camping" is mentioned, most people on Salt Spring immediately think of Ruckle Park. With 70 walk-in campsites near the water, it's a perfect place for tenters.

There are seven kilometres of shoreline to explore. Jayne Seagrave, author of bestselling *Provincial and National Park Campgrounds* and *BC's Best Camping Adventures*, ranks this as a favourite. Cyclist writer David Payne agrees. Jack Rosen points you to the beach in Grandma's Bay as "spectacular for intertidal viewing at low tide."

Ruckle Park Provincial Campsite.

The other public camping option is Mouat Park, right in Ganges, where there is a small but pleasant cluster of fifteen sites off Jackson Avenue. It usually fills up early during the summer. This is rumoured to be closing as we go to press. Privately run campsites are available at Lakeside Gardens and Cottage Resort.

Salt Spring's narrow roads are not inviting for large recreational vehicles and at present there is no public sani-dumping station available.

FRESHWATER FISHING

A number of island lakes are stocked annually, providing good angling year round. St. Mary Lake is well known for small-mouth bass, yielding the odd six-pounder. Some surrounding resorts sponsor a fishing derby every November. The lake also offers cutthroat and rainbow trout and steelhead.

Four other lakes provide good fishing spring to fall. Those with small boats will find launches on Cusheon, Stowell, and Weston Lakes and cutthroat trout awaiting you. (Only electric boat motors are allowed.) Weston has

some good-sized rainbows. A good place for the casual angler is Blackburn Lake, where a small fishing float sits at the end of a short lane beside the Fulford-Ganges Road. Both cutthroats and small-mouth bass provide the entertainment.

All anglers over sixteen must have a fishing licence. They can be purchased at most marinas and Mouat's Hardware.

SALTWATER FISHING

This is salmon country and in spite of declining stocks, sports fishers still enjoy the thrill of hooking into a spring, sockeye, pink, or chinook salmon during the season. Cod, halibut, and sole are also taken here. Several local businesses offer boat rentals and fishing charters to visitors

OTHER ACTIVITIES

Bird-watchers are treated to a varied resident population of birds. The Gulf Islands are on a major fly-way for migrating birds, too. Ruckle Park, Drummond Park, Beddis Beach, the Walker Hook area, and Southey Point all harbour shorebird colonies (see *Birds of Saltspring*).

Crabbing is another island secret generally reserved for locals who are out in force from fall to spring when the water is coolest. On the falling tide, crabbers can scoop up the makings of a magnificent dinner. Ruckle Park, Beddis Beach, and Burgoyne Bay are popular spots. A staircase at the end of Baker Road allows access to Booth Bay, another favoured spot. At the south end of the island, crabbers can park at Drummond Park and wade the shallows of Fulford Harbour as the tide ebbs.

Ellie often watches both locals and her B&B guests hunt down dinner. She keeps a copy of Charlie White's *How to Catch Crabs* and a few pairs of communal gumboots handy for novices. "Two fresh-boiled crabs, a glass of chardonnay, and a little sunshine dancing off the harbour and they're automatic repeat customers," she says.

Golfers will thoroughly enjoy the nine-hole Salt Spring Island Golf Club, north of Ganges near Central, where head pro Gord Ferguson has overseen things for more than a decade. This charming piece of property was the original homestead of one of the island's first authors, Reverend E. F. Wilson, who wrote *Salt Spring Island* in 1895. His son Norman converted their farm to a golf course in the 1920s. The family home, Barnsbury, was the clubhouse until it burned in the mid-1960s.

The course is a sound par-36 test with two good par-5s and an interesting mix of greens. There are two sets of tees which adds variety for those who want to play eighteen holes. The fairways roll over a forgiving terrain and there are club cars and pull carts to rent. Greens fees are reasonable and they have a first-come, first-served policy for visitors. The course is open year-round and there is good food and cold beer at Mulligan's Restaurant in the small clubhouse.

A recent addition for the golfing crowd is Blackburn Meadows, south of Ganges. This charming layout will take a little time to mature and is a par-3 seasonal track that is ideal for family outings and beginners.

Horseback riding is an activity that can be more or less enjoyable depending on the professionalism of the stable. Salt Spring is fortunate to have Salt Spring Guided Rides, which offers variable length tours over an 800-acre area on the slopes of Mount Maxwell. Advance bookings for two to six people can be made by calling Caroline seven days a week, preferably in the evening, at (250) 537-5761. The trails cover both the high country and lowlands near isolated Lake Maxwell and include a tranquil section through virgin forest.

The Mushroom Hunt. There are no poisonous mushrooms on Salt Spring, but some are more palatable than others. Consume new varieties with caution. Different types are prominent from spring to late fall (see *The Mushroom Couple*).

Scenic boat cruises are a natural attraction for a place like Salt Spring, and the options vary with the season. Both motor cruising and sailing charters are generally available year-round.

Swimming at Vesuvius Beach in the summer is preferable to the polar bear swim conducted by local residents on New

Year's Day. Most everyone on Salt Spring has a favourite swimming hole, but nobody wants to tell the world. Jack Rosen points visitors to Baiders Beach (a.k.a. Erskine), but I suspect there is a site he isn't talking about. The many freshwater lakes offer a more welcoming temperature and each has its own appeal.

Tennis lovers can play year-round at Portlock Park where an inflatable bubble keeps the rain away in winter months. With four courts and lighting, it is home to the Salt Spring Tennis Association. Visitors are welcome and may phone 250-537-4243 during business hours to reserve bubble court times. There are no reservations for outdoor courts. Further south there is a public court behind the Fulford firehall, and the Fulford marina rents out its court at $5/hour.

For rainy days there are billiards, bowling, and fitness centres right in Ganges. Another interesting option is a new indoor climbing centre that can test your vertical skills. The "Wall" is a non-profit project coordinated by Jack Rosen and designed to promote safe climbing. This is an economical outing for all ages. Call the Community Society at 537-9971 for hours of operation.

Salt Spring, while not small at 180 square kilometres, is compact enough to allow ready access to all its recreational options. When you get where you are going, you will normally find facilities are clean and well maintained. Most of that maintenance is voluntary, the result of a common attitude about packing out the garbage you have created. It's a great habit to get into.

The Mushroom Couple

On Salt Spring, no matter what your current interest there always seems to be someone living here who is an expert in whatever you want to learn. This theory was recently confirmed when we met with Alex and Victoria Olchowecki. Alex is a retired botanist who taught at the University of Manitoba. His specialty was mycology. In other words, he is an expert at identifying fungi, including mushrooms. Wild mush-

Alex and Victoria Olchowecki

rooms are quite abundant on Salt Spring Island. The variety of interesting flavours and textures made us ask Alex which were his favourites and most important, how we could be sure we were not eating a poisonous mushroom. He assured us that there are no lethal mushrooms on Salt Spring; the worst that can happen is that a person could have an upset stomach for up to six hours. As for which ones to eat, he said, "It depends on how daring you want to be. Not that many good edible ones exist. Most are either bitter tasting or hard or tough to eat."

Alex then revealed the times at which his favourite eating mushrooms could be found. Late March and April are the best time for the morels, a "fine eating mushroom." Victoria piped in that their favourite way to cook morels is to sauté them by themselves or in a sauce which has been flavoured with a little soy sauce and just half a teaspoon of chopped green pepper.

By summer, even though conditions are dry, the giant "agaricus agustus" can be found, often just by the side of the road. Cooked in a little garlic and cream, these agaricus are delicious.

In late summer and sometimes July the boletus can be harvested. To identify these, think of umbrella-shaped caps. Alex explains the underside of the boletus "have cores where

Agaricus   **Chanterelle**   **Morel**   **Shaggymane**

spores are forming rather than gills." There are no deadly ones that look similar. Alex notes, "These mushrooms are not particularly flavourful. The most popular thing is to dry them." But they are abundant and are found near trees.

Chanterelles appear in late summer or early fall. Alex says they grow in association with certain tree species and with salal, of which there is an abundance on Salt Spring. "They are easy to recognize. There is nothing that you can confuse them with. They are safe, tasty, and they can be frozen or preserved.

In October and November, after the rains come, honey mushrooms become available (We knew there would be a positive side to rain). "Honey mushrooms grow in clumps, as many as one hundred mushrooms can be on one stump." They dry well and are tasty.

The hedgehog mushroom "is a peach colour like Chanterelles. It has spines under the cap, which is where the name comes from. Again, you won't confuse these with any others." Hedgehog mushrooms are stimulated to grow in cooler weather. They thrive in January, especially if it has snowed and melted.

No list of edible mushrooms would be complete, according to Alex, without the shaggymane on it. Its distinctive shape can be seen in spring, summer, and fall. However, Alex cautions there is a closely related edible mushroom that causes an adverse reaction for some people if consumed with alcohol. "The effect can occur even if the alcohol is consumed a day or two after ingesting the mushrooms. It produces a mild rash, but nothing serious."

The fact that Victoria is affected in this way does not seem to squelch her enthusiasm for cooking and eating the shaggymanes. As with all the mushrooms, Victoria feels the flavours are enhanced by cooking them in butter or olive oil with the addition of a little garlic. She adds dry sherry to the chanterelles if the sauce needs more flavour, or a little nutmeg. Honey mushrooms are enhanced by the addition of a little dill. But Victoria says, "We don't care to add onion, it's too sweet."

All mushrooms can be frozen to be preserved. "Clean with a mushroom brush under water. Heat in a little water and bring to a boil. With honey mushrooms I throw out the first water," states Victoria. "All the others I keep the water to freeze them in." They can be stored for great lengths of time with no ill effect.

Alex is a member of the British Mycological Society, which has a worldwide membership and produces a monthly research journal. Alex is a retired academic, but he says the Society has a lot of members who are not academics. In Britain, he points out, "natural history is loaded with amateur experts." They conduct forays into the forests all over Britain to collect and document what is collected. Alex adds, "The same mushrooms don't grow in the same place every year. Sometimes you won't have found one in a region for ten years. Sometimes you find species not before described." Alex explained that there must be "a sufficient difference between this and other species to warrant a new species."

The Olchoweckis had some hints for gathering mushrooms. "Pick clean. Cut mushrooms with a knife. Clean as you go along. Put the mushrooms in a bucket (not plastic), a basket, or paper bag. A basket would be ideal. Cut off the stem to check for maggots. If there are any, leave those. If you do this, you barely need to rinse when you get home." And remember, no matter how enthusiastic you become, it is always common courtesy not to pick mushrooms on private land.

BIRDS OF SALT SPRING

The soothing landscape and mild temperate climate of Salt Spring do not only attract people to visit or take up residence. Our island home is also crowded with feathered friends from the tiny rufous hummingbird to the soaring bald eagle.

At any time of the year you can watch a veritable avian circus at the bird feeders found in almost every yard. The dark-eyed "Oregon" juncos in their black, brown, and white array often vie for seeds with flocks of rose-coloured house and purple finches, while chestnut-backed chickadees and red-breasted nuthatches dash in like bandits and steal a tasty sunflower seed.

In the brush under trees and hedges, the rustle of kicked-up leaves often heralds the presence of a rufous-sided towhee, whose beady red eye will transfix you if you look too closely. Another ground feeder unique to the west is the varied thrush. This rusty-coloured bird has an unusual and eerie quavering call that echoes through the cedar trees. A more recognizable bird of the thrush family is the American robin, familiar to anyone in North America. Not so familiar, however, is watching flocks

STEVE COOPMAN

A professional theatre director, administrator, and educator in Ontario for twenty years, Steve Coopman moved west to get closer to nature. With an abiding interest in the outdoors since he was a child, Steve has taken great delight in acquainting himself with birds of the west since arriving on Salt Spring three years ago. This avid amateur ornithologist contributed this piece.

A variety of waterfowl can always be found enjoying Fulford Harbour.

of robins cluster in the arbutus trees in the late fall to feast on the bunches of bright red berries that festoon the branches of this evergreen deciduous tree.

Our tiniest aviator is the rufous hummingbird. In early spring, large numbers of "hummers" visit the island and it is a treat to watch their antics, particularly around feeders. These small birds are fiercely territorial, and they defend their nectar sources with reckless abandon, often swooping down in noisy attack to chase off interlopers. At this time of year the males are in residence. You'll recognize them by their cedar-coloured side and back feathers and incredibly iridescent throats.

Perhaps the most comical bird on the island is the California quail. This diminutive member of the gallinaceous, or fowl-like bird family can be found in most areas of the island. You will see long lines of tiny baby quail bookended by mom and dad, travelling on furiously moving little legs and looking like toy locomotives undulating through the underbrush or across the narrow country lanes. With their bobbing feathered plumes, these fat little residents look like they scurried straight out of a Walt Disney cartoon.

Other bird characters on Salt Spring include the northwestern crow, a sub-species specific to the northwestern coast, the raucous Steller's jay, and the startling piliated woodpecker. The crows here cruise the beaches looking for tasty tidbits. When they find a clam, they take it to a nearby road or driveway and drop it from a respectable height to crack open the packaging on their dinner. Steller's jays like the shady wooded areas of fir and cedar. Their rasping call can be heard from quite a distance, and when they visit a feeder they seem to take delight in emptying as much out of it in as short a time as possible. They fling their magnificently crested heads back and forth, the dusky blue and black feathers that cover them making quite an impact. The piliated woodpecker, otherwise known as the "cock of the North" and sounding much like Woody Woodpecker, swoops through the woods looking for rotting trees with plenty of good bugs under the bark. The size of a crow and with a flaming red crest, he's hard to miss.

We have plenty of birds of prey in the air around Salt Spring including owls, hawks, vultures, and of course bald eagles. When the salmon are running through Active Pass, there are sometimes so many eagles they look like a flock of crows, but there's no mistaking that white head and tail and the huge yellow beak. You can see an occasional osprey diving for its dinner in one of our numerous lakes, and if you're lucky at dusk you may hear a rasping hiss and look up to see a ghostly barn owl drift past on silent wings. During hot summer days the Fulford Valley is a great place to watch birds of prey riding the thermals along the sides of the valley and up the face of Mount Maxwell.

For birders interested in waterfowl, the ocean around the island teems with gulls, ducks, cormorants, loons, and geese. At low tide the end of Fulford Harbour is sometimes so crowded with waterfowl it is difficult to see the mud flats. St. Mary Lake is also an excellent place to study birds. Salt Spring is on the western fly-route, and many migrating flocks drop down to the lake for a night or longer. You'll often see American coots and common goldeneye, as well as the occasional pair of trumpeter swans. The shores of the lake are also home to many red-winged blackbirds during the summer.

The residents of Salt Spring treasure our avian neighbours. In 1997, the Wild Bird Trust raised money to purchase a tract of land on the island that is home to the biggest colony of great blue herons in the Gulf Islands. The Heronry has become a source of pride for birders here, and we all look forward to watching many generations of herons hatch and grow to healthy adulthood in their new home.

For serious bird-watchers, Salt Spring is an excellent place to spend a few days adding some sightings of birds unique to this part of the world. For travellers interested in the overall experience of visiting our island paradise, you cannot help but notice the abundance of life in all its forms that crowds the land, the sea, and the air of Salt Spring.

8

AN
ACCOMMODATING PLACE

FOR ALL OF ITS TOURIST APPEAL AND WIDESPREAD recognition as a cultural destination, Salt Spring has no dominant hotel or destination resort. In fact, there is no facility with more than 30 rooms available. Small is beautiful and here it is the diversity of B&Bs and lakeside resorts that are the attraction.

In a sense the island's hospitality industry is an extension of its culture. The proposal of a megaproject has faced extensive resistance.

The following provides both insight into the makeup of Salt Spring's leading industry as well as specific details on an assortment of attractive accommodations from a five-star country inn to a tree house at a hostel.

AN ISLAND OF B&Bs

The numerous Bed & Breakfasts on Salt Spring are as unique and varied as the people operating them. The common characteristics shared by the hosts are their interest in meeting people from all over the world and their pleasure at being able to share their piece of "island paradise."

Many of our Bed & Breakfast owners have decided to call Salt Spring home after searching far and wide for their chosen place.

Betsy Johnston and Derek Hill, from Anchorage Cove B&B, looked all around the coastal area including Vancouver Island and many Gulf Islands. By luck they came to Salt Spring for a day. Here they found their dream property and built a new home with plans to operate a B&B. Having operated Old Notch Farm Inn in Quebec for three years, they are seasoned operators. With their experience they were able to create a very guest-friendly home.

Susan Evans and Ted Harrison of Weston Lake Inn enjoyed cycling and kayaking in the Gulf Islands as early as 1985. They shared a dream to come to the country, but always believed it would be many years before they could realize that dream. While on Salt Spring during a cycling trip, they made an offer on a property, which much to their surprise was accepted. Immediately they had to reorganize their lives drastically so they could develop this dream property. To capitalize on the Expo'86 tourist market, Susan left her job to live on Salt Spring and operate a B&B. Ted continued to commute to his city job for eight years but now enjoys retirement and operates a charter sailing business, "Welcome Aboard." Weston Lake Inn was one of the earliest B&Bs on the island. Olive Layard at Kitchener House claims she was number seven when she started in 1987.

Ellen Karpinski of Salt Spring Way is originally from Detroit, Michigan. After living in Canada for a few years she moved to Colorado, but after four years was anxious to return to Canada. When they left the rural lifestyle of Colorado, Ellen and her husband, Jerry, set forth to find a house suitable for a B&B on Salt Spring.

In April 1988, Patti and Dick Stubbs visited the island to look for property. At that time, all ten existing B&Bs were fully occupied. Seeing this shortage of accommodation on the island, they designed their new home and were operating their own B&B, Becton Croft, by year's end. They were not alone. In that short timespan twenty other entrepreneurs embraced the same idea. The Salt Spring B&B boom was happening.

The supply of rooms was matched by a growing demand—especially in the summer months. Fortunately for tourists, the standards of many pioneer B&Bs on Salt Spring were high and this has helped maintain the quality within the local industry.

Still, each B&B has unique traits or specialties that appeal to different people. Some are more attuned to families, pet policies differ, a few emphasize gourmet breakfasts as a draw, others promote location and amenities.

We have opted to highlight about a third of the current operators. We established a general criteria based on a number of standards such as: hosts' experience, amenities, quality of accommodation (queen-size beds were treated as the standard), breakfast facilities, special offerings, rate structure, plus intangibles that simply come with knowing the island and its people.

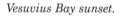

In 1994, Ellie did inspections on numerous Gulf Island B&Bs for Tourism BC's "Approved Accommodation" Guide program. Acceptance to this guide is based on standards of courtesy, comfort, and cleanliness and we have used the same criteria for inclusion here. All facilities listed are open year-round, and B&B operators must have a minimum of two years' experience.

A frustration of innkeepers is the casual judgment occasionally offered by guidebook "researchers" who make assessments from the driveway. Curb appeal is important, but we want you to know what lies beyond the entrance. Ellie has viewed the interior and interviewed the hosts of all B&B properties listed.

Rates quoted are for the 1998 peak season based on double occupancy and are subject to change in later years. Inquire about weekly or off-season rates or rates for additional persons.

Note: Please ask individual operators about their pet policies. In some instances owners have acute animal allergies which influence their policies. These restrictions must be respected by guests.

We welcome reader comments on their experience at Salt Spring B&Bs. Contact us either by regular mail or e-mail via our publisher (herhouse@island.net). More accommodation listings are available from Salt Spring's Tourist Information Centre at (250) 537-5252 or fax (250) 537-4276.

Vesuvius Bay sunset.

AMBLECOTE

AMBLECOTE
Bed & Breakfast

Hosts:	Paul Gravett & Mark Hand
	132 Isle View Drive, SSI V8K 2G4
Phone:	(250) 537-1205
Fax:	(250) 537-1205
E-mail:	isleview@saltspring.com
Units:	1 **Rates:** $105

FEATURE: AN ELEGANT SUITE OFFERING PRIVACY AND AN EXPANSIVE OCEAN VIEW. OPENED 1997.

Amblecote, named after the English village where Mark's ancestors lived, provides its guests with an elegant, two-room, private suite on the ground level of the house. The four-poster bed and a fine selection of antiques create an atmosphere of old English charm.

Breakfast is served on the upper floor in the hosts' dining room, which features an expansive view of the outer islands. Established flowering shrubs and huge arbutus trees afford guests a feeling of tranquillity and privacy in the adjacent outdoor hot tub, which shares the same spectacular view. Mark and Paul owned and operated Amblecote B&B in Toronto for five years prior to moving to Salt Spring. Bringing their experience with them, they have done extensive renovations to their new domain, making it an inviting place for guests to enjoy.

Guest Comments: *An oasis for my soul. Wonderful accommodation, delicious breakfasts.*

Smoked Salmon with Eggs in Puff Pastry with Hollandaise Sauce

8 large eggs	2 tbsp butter
2 tbsp each chopped red and green bell peppers	
2 tbsp sour cream	4-6 tbsp chopped smoked salmon
4 puff pastry shells	hollandaise sauce (see page 177)

Beat eggs until light and fluffy. In a frying pan melt butter. Add peppers. Saute until just barely limp. Add eggs, cooking and stirring until almost done. Add sour cream and salmon. Stir. Do not let eggs get too dry, but remove from heat while still creamy. Spoon eggs and salmon into each pastry shell. Cover with 2 to 3 tablespoons of hollandaise sauce and garnish with one or two salmon slices. Serves 4.

Anchorage Cove

Hosts: Betsy Johnston & Derek Hill
449 Long Harbour Road, SSI V8K 2M2
Phone: (250) 537-5337 or 1-888-537-5360
Fax: (250) 537-5360
E-mail: betsyderek@saltspring.com
Units: 3 **Rates:** $115 - $135

FEATURE: OCEANFRONT WEST COAST CONTEMPORARY HOME WITH PRIVATE MOORAGE IN GANGES HARBOUR. HOT TUB ON THE DOCK. OPENED 1996.

You can arrive at this spectacular setting by boat or vehicle. Two of the rooms directly face the harbour with expansive views of the ocean. All rooms have en suites and the Arbutus Room can be made up with king or twin beds.

Guests enjoy a private entrance to the guest lounge, which looks south onto the open harbour toward Goat Island and the Chain Islands. It features a woodstove, pool table, pine antiques, a cozy sitting area, and a stocked galley of hot beverages.

Having operated Old Notch Farm Inn in Quebec, Betsy and Derek came to Salt Spring Island to open Anchorage Cove in 1996 as experienced B&B hosts.

Guest Comments: *Great food and beautiful surroundings made for an enjoyable stay, but it was the friendly atmosphere that will bring us back. L&J, Aurora, Ontario.*

Smoked Salmon Strata

1/3 cup softened herb cream cheese	12 slices egg bread
2 minced green onions	12 slices smoked salmon
2 cups milk	4 eggs
1/4 tsp each dried dillweed and pepper	2 tsp Dijon mustard
1/2 cup shredded Swiss cheese	chopped green onions

Prepare at least 4 hours or the night before. Spread cream cheese over bread, sprinkle half of bread slices with minced green onion, top evenly with smoked salmon. Top with remaining bread slices, cheese side down, cut in half diagonally. Arrange in 13- x 9-inch baking dish or in individual ramekins. In bowl whisk together milk, eggs, mustard, dillweed, pepper, and pour evenly over strata. Sprinkle with Swiss cheese. Cover with plastic wrap and refrigerate for at least 4 hours. Let stand at room temperature for 30 minutes. Bake in 350° F oven for about 35 minutes or until set and lightly golden. Garnish with chopped green onion. Serves 6-8.

ANNIE'S
OCEANFRONT HIDEAWAY

Hosts: Rick & Ruth-Anne Broad
168 Simson Road, SSI V8K 1E2
Phone: (250) 537-0851 or 1-888-474-2663
Fax: (250) 537-0861
E-mail: annes@saltspring.com
Units: 4   **Rates:** $175-$210

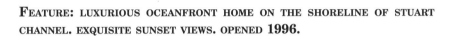

FEATURE: LUXURIOUS OCEANFRONT HOME ON THE SHORELINE OF STUART CHANNEL. EXQUISITE SUNSET VIEWS. OPENED 1996.

Rick and Ruth-Anne designed their B&B with guests' needs in mind. Each room is decorated with a pleasing colour scheme and luxurious furnishings. Ocean views, hydro-massage tubs, and separate heat and air controls are added features.

The rooms are named for tree species on view. The Garry Oak Room, dubbed the "Special Occasion Room," contains a large in-room tub surrounded by mirrors, double shower, canopy bed, fireplace, and panoramic ocean view. An in-house elevator provides wheelchair access to the Douglas Fir Room. A breakfast to surpass all expectations is served in the grand guest dining room. An outdoor hot tub, exercise room, and beach access are additional amenities for guests to enjoy.

Guest Comments: *I feel as though transported by angels to a part of heaven...My mind, body, and soul thank you. D.L. Victoria, B.C.*

crab Quiche Tarts

1 tbsp butter	1/2 cup finely chopped green onions
4-6 oz shredded cooked crab	1/4 cup finely chopped parsley
pinch of white pepper	1-1/4 cups cream (or half & half)
5 lightly beaten eggs	1 tsp Dijon mustard
1/4 tsp salt	1 cup grated Monterey Jack cheese
1/4 tsp paprika	24 tart shells

Cook onions until softened, remove from heat. Cool. Add crab, parsley, and white pepper. Stir. Combine eggs, cream, and spices with onion-crab mixture. Stir well. Pour into tart shells. Sprinkle grated Monterey Jack cheese on top. Bake at 450°F for 10 minutes. Reduce to 350°F and bake for another 20-25 minutes. Makes 24 tarts.

The Beach House

Host: Ellie Thorburn
369 Isabella Point Road, SSI V8K 1V4
Phone: (250) 653-2040 or 1-888-653-6334
Fax: (250) 653-9711
Units: 3 (one unit sleeps 5)   **Rates:** $120 - $140

FEATURE: LOCATED RIGHT ON FULFORD HARBOUR WITH MAGNIFICENT VIEWS, GREAT SUNRISES (SEE BOOK COVER!), AND AN OCEANSIDE OUTDOOR HOT TUB. OPENED 1990.

Ellie's personal touches mark any stay at The Beach House. In two new suites at the water's edge, guests wake to the morning tide lapping at the doorstep. Regular visitors return in all seasons. The one-bedroom Sunrise Suite, with full kitchen, can accommodate a family. The adult-oriented Starfish Room with an in-room jacuzzi tub and the Sand Dollar Room are tastefully appointed. In the bright sunroom or on the oceanside deck revelling in the morning sun, guests enjoy a full breakfast. Easy access to the beach allows guests to beachcomb at low tides. In the cooler months, clam digging and crabbing are pleasant activities.

Additional amenities include gas barbecue, on-site laundry, hot beverage bar, an outdoor fire-pit, and outdoor hot tub looking onto the harbour. Each unit has its own private entrance.

Guest Comments: *For the past 51 weeks we lived in reality; the past week we've lived in paradise...The early morning sunrise, the waves lapping peacefully against the shoreline, and the swans sailing by made for the most idyllic time we've ever encountered. Thank you for sharing.*

"Berry" Special

Place fresh or frozen raspberries in their juices with a few drops of lemon juice. Puree a banana, flavoured with a hint of nutmeg.

Fill a large parfait glass or wine goblet with the berries. Just before serving, pour the pureed banana into the glass, allowing the banana to seep through the berries. Sprinkle lightly with cinnamon sugar and garnish with sliced kiwi.

Note: This works well with any fresh or frozen fruit such as strawberries, peaches, blackberries, etc. Strawberry and peach are very popular.

BECTON CROFT

Host: Patti & Dick Stubbs
121 Elizabeth Drive, SSI V8K 1H8
Phone: (250) 537-4784
Units: 2   **Rates:** $59

FEATURE: WITHIN WALKING DISTANCE OF THE VESUVIUS FERRY, STORE, AND PUB. OPENED 1988.

Becton Croft offers attractive accommodation overlooking pastoral views of a nearby hobby farm. The guest rooms are located in a separate building beside the house and each has a private entrance. Don't be fooled by the affordable rates; the rooms are clean, comfortable, and private, with en suite baths. A continental breakfast is delivered to your room. The name Becton Croft derives from Dick's family heritage, Becton Rough and Meadow Croft. Since opening the business in 1988, Patti and Dick have made numerous friends at their B&B, many of whom return for regular visits and have welcomed the Stubbs in their own homes in distant places.

Guest Comments: *Best kept secret on Salt Spring Island. Great place to get engaged—we'll be back.*

Apple Kiwi Muffins

Mix together:
1-1/2 cups flour
2 tsp baking powder
1/2 tsp salt

1 cup wild oats (instant)
1 tsp baking soda

Beat well:
1 egg
1/2 cup milk
1 cup mashed kiwis and apple sauce

1/4 cup oil
1/2 cup brown sugar

Fold ingredients together. Don't overmix. For 6 extra large muffins, bake at 400°F for 22 minutes. For 12 regular muffins, bake at 400° F for 15 minutes.

Beddis House

Hosts: Bev & Terry Bolton
131 Miles Avenue, SSI V8K 2E1
Phone: (250) 537-1028
Fax: (250) 537-9888
E-mail: beddis@saltspring.com
Units: 3   **Rates:** $150 - $180

Feature: this restored historical farmhouse built in 1900 is nestled between the sea and a heritage apple orchard. opened 1995.

Beyond the garden gate, an inviting hammock beckons. Gravel pathways, lined with English border gardens, lead to both the main house and the adjacent Coach House, which the Boltons built to accommodate their B&B guests. Consistent with the décor of the original farmhouse, each room is furnished with antiques, a woodstove, and an en suite bathroom featuring a claw foot tub and shower.

The Rose Bower Room features a cherrywood four-poster, king-size bed and armoire. A private balcony offers a view of the ever-changing scenes on Ganges Harbour.

Guest Comments: *Outstanding! Where do we start? Warm and interesting hosts with a mind to the little touches, good food well presented, a luxurious room tastefully decorated, all set in an idyllic spot. Bravo! Calgary, Alberta.*

Apple Puff Pancakes

Our heritage apple trees produce so many apples they are often featured on menus at Beddis House.

6 apples, peeled, cored, and sliced	9 eggs
scant 1/2 cup margarine or butter	1-1/2 cups milk
1-1/2 cups all-purpose flour	3 tsp almond extract
1/4 tsp salt	

Heat convection oven to 425°F, regular oven to 450°F. Saute the apples in butter and divide among 3 greased, glass, 8-inch pie plates. With mixer, beat together eggs, add flour gradually, then milk, extract, and salt. Beat well and pour evenly over apples. Bake 20 minutes until puffed and brown. Sprinkle with confectioner's sugar. Cut each pancake into quarters and serve 2 quarters on a warmed plate. Garnish with twisted orange slices and serve with warm maple syrup. Serves 6.

BLACKBERRY

Hosts: Linda Ritchie & Jamie Alexander
210 Stewart Road, SSI V8K 2C4
Phone: (250) 537-5626
Units: 3 **Rates:** $75 - $95

— Bed & Breakfast —

FEATURE: FRIENDLY, HELPFUL HOSTS CREATE A WARM, CASUAL ATMOSPHERE. OPENED 1991.

A quiet hillside setting with distant mountain and water views, comfortable rooms with private entrances, and a hot tub draw guests to Blackberry. Room 1 is the room with a view, four-poster pine bed, and en suite bathroom. Room 3 with a queen bed and Room 2 with a double, sharing a hallway bathroom, provide very affordable accommodation for guests wanting separate beds or a party of three travelling together. Esme, born July 1996, is the pride and joy of her delighted parents and a welcome addition to Blackberry—not to slight the resident dogs, Ziggy and Zappa. Families welcome by pre-arrangement.

Guest Comment: *Linda is the best cook and Jamie is a good servant. Jonathon, age 8.*

Carrot or Zucchini Muffins

1/2 cup flour	1/2 cup natural wheat bran
1/2 cup oat bran	1 tbsp baking powder
1 tsp cinnamon	1/2 tsp nutmeg
1/2 cup brown sugar	1 egg
1/2 cup milk	1/4 cup vegetable oil
1/2 cup raisins	1-1/2 cups finely grated carrot or zucchini

In a large bowl combine flour, brans, baking powder, and spices. Blend in brown sugar until no lumps remain. In small bowl beat together egg, milk, oil, and carrots or zucchini. Pour all at once over dry ingredients, sprinkle with raisins. Don't overmix. Spoon into 8 greased muffin cups. Bake 350°F for about 25 minutes.

CAPTAIN'S PASSAGE

Hosts: Bob & Lauretta Wilson
1510 Beddis Road, SSI V8K 2E3
Phone: (250) 537-9469
Fax: (250) 537-9463
Units: 2 **Rates:** $80 - $90

FEATURE: PANORAMIC VIEW OF CAPTAIN'S PASSAGE AND PREVOST ISLAND. OPENED 1990.

A cedar, West Coast style home perched among fir and cedar trees, Captain's Passage has a real coastal island appeal. The nautical theme starts at the driveway entrance. Each of the two guest rooms features a wide-angle view across treetops to the surrounding waterways and outer islands. En suite shower bathrooms and comfortable sitting areas are included with each room. The Welbury Bay Room offers a choice of king or twin beds. There is also a guest lounge with woodstove, library, and a large bay window facing the spectacular view. Breakfast is served in the comfortable dining room.

Guest comments: *Perfection down to the smallest details combined with warm hospitality. Breakfasts worth getting up for.*

BC Peach Pancakes

2-1/2 cups all purpose flour	6 tsp baking powder
2 tbsp sugar	1 tsp salt
4 eggs	1-1/2 cups milk or 1/3 cup peach juice
1/4 cup melted butter	1 16 oz can peaches, chopped
cinnamon to taste	1/2 cup raisins soaked in rum or juice

Combine dry ingredients. Add eggs and butter and slowly add enough milk to achieve a thick batter. Add peaches and raisins if used. In a skillet, heat a small amount of butter, ladle in batter, and cook until golden on each side. Serve with fruit or maple syrup. Serves 6.

CRANBERRY RIDGE

Host: Gloria Callison-Lutz
269 Don Ore Drive, SSI V8K 2H5
Phone: (250) 537-4854 or 1-888-537-4854
Fax: (250) 537-4854
Units: 3 **Rates:** $100 - $150

FEATURE: VIEW OF THE OUTER ISLANDS, REACHING TO THE NORTH SHORE MOUNTAINS AND THE LIGHTS OF VANCOUVER. EASTERN EXPOSURE CAPTURES SPECTACULAR SUNRISES. OPENED **1990.**

A contemporary home, Cranberry Ridge was designed to operate as a B&B. Gloria assures the friendly arrival of early morning coffee and juice at your door. Her love for decorating and crafts is apparent in every room.

Three guest rooms, each appointed in its own style, take advantage of the view. The Twig Room, the most luxurious, features a fireplace, willow furniture, privacy, and en suite bath with jacuzzi tub. The Country Room's king-size bed can be converted to twins for a minimum two-night stay. A third bed is also available. Chickadee pine furniture, wall stencilling, and patchwork quilts accent the country theme. The en suite bath also has a jacuzzi tub. A common guest area is stocked with hot beverages, goodies, and a bar fridge. The outdoor hot tub on the deck is an added bonus. (Dogs on approval for an additional charge of $20.)

Guest Comments: *We left with a contented feeling and a spring in our step. The Twig Room is beautiful. D&E.*

Cranberry Ridge Biscotti

Pour 1 cup hot water over 1 cup dried cranberries. Set aside.

Combine 2 eggs	3/4 cup sugar
1/2 cup oil	2 tsp orange zest
1 tsp cinnamon	1-1/4 tsp baking powder
1/2 tsp almond extract	1/4 tsp salt
Add: 2 cups flour	1 cup coarsely chopped almonds
Drained cranberries	

Form into a shape 3 inches wide, 3/4 inch thick, and however long. Sprinkle with sugar before baking at 350°F for 30 minutes. Cool for 10 minutes and cut into 1-inch slices. Return to oven for 15 minutes.

DEMERY'S RETREAT

Hosts: Jennifer & George Demery
471 Sky Valley Road, SSI V8K 2C3
Phone: (250) 537-0015
Fax: (250) 537-0015
E-mail: demery@saltspring.com
Units: 1   **Rates:** $75 - $90

FEATURE: NESTLED ON 3.5 ACRES OF NATURAL LANDSCAPING, THIS IS A PEACEFUL SETTING WHERE DEER ARE REGULAR VISITORS. OPENED 1996.

A warm welcome immediately makes guests feel at home. On the upper floor, the cheery Lookout Room is decorated in French country blues and yellows and has its own balcony. The Wildflower Room décor features hand-painted wildflowers on the walls of the bathroom. A guest lounge provides a fireplace, hot beverage bar, and a bird's eye view of the deer feeding at the backyard pond. The Demerys create a folksy atmosphere which is their calling card.

Guest Comments: *Great food, great place, great bed, great people! Thanks. David Blake, England.*

Sweet Pepper and Onion Frittata

1/4 cup plus 2 tbsp olive oil	2 cups thinly sliced onions
2 or 3 garlic cloves, minced	1-1/2 cups julienned red sweet peppers
1/4 cup chopped fresh basil	8 eggs
1/2 tsp salt or to taste	3 tbsp light cream (or half and half)
Freshly ground black pepper	2 tbsp butter
1/3 cup freshly grated Parmesan cheese	

Heat 1/4 cup of olive oil in large skillet over low heat. Add onions and peppers, cook until tender and slightly caramelized, about 35 to 45 minutes. Stir in garlic and basil. Remove from heat.

In a bowl, beat eggs, light cream, cheese. Add salt and pepper.

Over medium heat, melt 1 tbsp butter and 1 tbsp oil in non-stick skillet, add the onion and pepper mixture. Pour the egg mixture over the vegetables. On low heat, cook until the eggs are set around the edges. Gently lift the edges of the omelette with a spatula and tilt the pan to let the uncooked egg run underneath. Continue cooking until the eggs have set on top. Place a plate over the top of the pan and invert, turning the frittata onto the plate. Add the remaining 1 tbsp butter and oil to the pan and slide the frittata back into the pan, cooked side up. Cook until the bottom is set, 2 to 3 minutes.

Place a preheated plate over the pan, invert, and turn the frittata out onto the plate. Cut into wedges and serve hot.

KITCHENER HOUSE

Host: Olive Layard
166 Booth Road, SSI V8K 2M8
Phone: (250) 537-9879
Units: 3 plus cottage   **Rates:** $65 - $135

FEATURE: EXTENSIVE WOODLAND GARDENS, WITH HOUSE OVERLOOKING BOOTH CANAL. VIEWS FACE WEST TO THE OUTER HARBOUR FROM THIS SECLUDED LOCATION. OPENED **1987**.

Once you open the tall, deer-proof, cedar slat gates (and don't forget to close them), you are drawn through English country gardens toward a charming home on the shoreline. The whole place exudes a warm, carefree atmosphere. Olive, an avid gardener and artist with a long history on Salt Spring Island, is a true conversationalist. Her high spirits bring guests back to Kitchener House time and time again. Visitors seek out this oasis to gather some horticultural tips. Olive has been known to share cuttings and seeds as well. The en suite room on the lowest level features French doors leading to a private, waterside deck. Two upper rooms, one with twin beds and the other a single, share the host bathroom. The cedar country kitchen features a large woodstove and is a natural gathering spot to experience island hospitality.

The luxurious one-bedroom cottage is self-contained, fully appointed, and a superb piece of workmanship, but be sure to reserve early for this treasure (weekly rate, $850).

Guest Comments: *Thank you for the lovely hospitality and delicious breakfasts. The garden and the house are a joy for eyes and soul. Thank you Olive.*

Country stove—a feature of Kitchener House.

Log House

Hosts: Wayne & Doreen Hewitt
490 Horel Road, SSI V8K 2C6
Phone: (250) 537-1104
Fax: (250) 537-1781
E-mail: loghouse@saltspring.com
Units: 2   **Rates:** $70 - $80

FEATURE: PRIVATE BEACH ACCESS ON CUSHEON LAKE, ANTIQUE LIGHT FIXTURES, AND A HERITAGE STAIRCASE FROM VICTORIA. OPENED **1995.**

For log house lovers, this is the place to stay. The Rose Room has a skylight above the bed and a private bath next door. The Ivy Room on the main floor is beside the guest lounge. The bathroom is adjacent to the kitchen, and robes are provided for guests. There is an on-deck hot tub. The guest lounge features a stone fireplace and overlooks the lake. Canoes and sailboats are provided for guest use. The breakfast menu offers a varied choice. A great place to wake up in the morning. (Children six years and older welcome.)

Guest Comments: *The house is beautiful and cozy, surroundings wonderful. The hosts are so helpful, going out of their way all the time to ensure that everything is to your satisfaction. The food is superb and lots of helpful info about things to do on the island. Thank you everyone. Best of luck in the future! Vancouver, B.C.*

Log House Menu

Light-Hearted Breakfast
Juice, muffins, scones, or fruit loaf
Fresh fruit plate
Coffee, tea, milk

Loggers Breakfast
Fruit juice
Fruit plate or fruit salad
Muffins, scones, coffee
cake, or fruit loaf
Waffles, pancakes, or French toast
Maple syrup or fruit sauces
Coffee, tea, milk

Humpty Dumpty Special
Juice
Fruit plate or fruit salad
Muffins, scones, coffee
cake, or fruit loaf
Poached eggs, scrambled egg,
omelette, quiche, or ham
Toast with jam
Coffee, tea, milk

THE PARTRIDGE HOUSE

Host: Lynne Partridge
131 Salt Spring Way, SSI V8K 2G3
Phone: (250) 537-2822
Fax: (250) 537-1443
E-mail: partridge@saltspring.com
Units: 2   **Rates:** $65 - $85

FEATURE: PANORAMIC VIEW OF THE OUTER ISLANDS AND ACTIVE PASS—ON A CLEAR DAY YOU CAN SEE THE NORTH SHORE MOUNTAINS. OPENED 1993.

The Partridge House offers ideal family accommodation if you book the whole floor. The Studio Suite houses a queen bed, a kitchenette, and a spacious sitting area with a queen sofa bed, woodstove, and TV. The adjacent bathroom also services the Blue Room, which has a twin bed and a double bed. The décor is pleasant, and the outdoor hot tub boasts the same spectacular view as the rooms. Hot beverages, bar refrigerators, guest robes, library, board games, and information guides are additional touches provided in each room.

Guest Comments: *Salt Spring is a place to "step off," quiet, slower, beautiful, and everyone we met was helpful and friendly. Your place is a perfect retreat, filled with wonderful thoughtful touches, fluffy towels, good bed, and to-die-for breakfast. J and J, Redmond, WA.*

Cheese Souffle

Place a pan with about 1 inch of water in oven, and set to 325° F.
Melt 4 tbsp butter. Blend in 4 tbsp flour. Add gradually 1 cup milk
Stir until thick and smooth. Add 1/2 tsp salt. 1/4 tsp cayenne, and 1 cup grated cheddar cheese. Stir until smooth and remove from heat.
Add 4 egg yolks, beaten until light.
Cool. Just before baking, beat 4 eggs whites until stiff (5 for a fluffier souffle).

Stir a tablespoon of the egg white into the sauce mixture. Gradually fold in the rest. Spoon into an unbuttered 1-1/2 quart straight-sided dish. Set in the pan of hot water. Bake 45 minutes. Serve immediately.

Looking out on Booth Canal from the deckside garden of Kitchener House B&B.

The Beach House B&B on Fulford Harbour.

Welbury Bay Room at Captain's Passage B&B provides a view of Prevost Island.

Beddis House B&B is a restored heritage house built in 1900.

Anne's Oceanfront Hideway overlooking Stuart Channel.

Log House B&B on Cusheon Lake.

Seaside gardens at Anchorage Cove B&B.

Enjoy the beautiful gardens and ocean views from the deck at Summerhill Guest House.

Twig Room at Cranberry Ridge B&B features a fireplace and views of the outer islands.

Water's Edge B&B on Ganges Harbour.

THE SALT SPRING WAY

Hosts: Ellen Karpinski & Jerry Barenholtz
100 Salt Spring Way, SSI V8K 2G8
Phone: (250) 537-5087
Fax: (250) 537-1797
E-mail: thesaltspringway@saltspring.com
Units: 2   **Rates:** $65 - $75

FEATURE: SECLUSION AND PRIVACY WITH A GREAT VIEW OF OCEAN, ISLANDS AND NORTH SHORE MOUNTAINS. OPENED 1993.

The Salt Spring Way exemplifies the ambience of the island—relaxed, casual hospitality in a warm, friendly atmosphere. The Mountain Room and Island Room, each with views, share a bathroom (with shower only) down the hall. A common sitting area offers cable TV, stereo, beverage bar, library, and games. Tub lovers can lounge in an outdoor hot tub, which is set aside from the house in a private area that captures the view at its best.

When designing her B&B, Ellen at first considered a separate guest dining room for breakfast. Instead she decided to serve guests breakfast in her own dining area to make them feel more welcome. As a hostess, Ellen has a special knack for making guests feel at home. Resident cats and pet sheep share the reception.

Guest Comments: *Not just sublime, but also sumptuous and superlative! Vancouver.*

Spinach Feta Cheese Omelette

1 cup washed spinach leaves
3 eggs
Dash of hot pepper sauce
Fresh herbs
2 tsp butter

3 slices feta cheese
1 tbsp water
salt and pepper
1/4 cup chopped onion
2 tsp olive oil

Using a 10-inch non-stick skillet, saute onion in 1 tsp butter and 1 tsp oil. Roughly chop spinach and add to onion, sauteing until limp. Remove spinach and onion to a small plate. Beat eggs with water and hot pepper sauce, salt, and pepper.

Melt 1 tsp butter and 1 tsp oil in same pan. Roughly chop fresh herbs and stir into butter. Pour in egg mixture. Shake to distribute herbs. Pull up edges to allow liquid to go under cooked part.

Lay thin slices of feta cheese on half of the omelette. Top cheese with spinach mixture. Fold plain side over cheese and spinach and serve.

Summerhill Guest House

Hosts: Paul Eastman & Michael McLandress
209 Chu-an Drive, SSI V8K 1H9
Phone: (250) 537-2727
Fax: (250) 537-4301
E-mail: summerhill@saltspring.com
Units: 3   **Rates:** $95 - $120

FEATURE: HIGH-BANK WATERFRONT HOME NESTLED AMONG ARBUTUS TREES ON A LARGE LOT AFFORDS A TRUE FEELING OF PRIVACY. OPENED 1993.

Discovering Summerhill is a real treat for island visitors. As part of the extensive renovations which Paul and Michael have done, the upper floor was redesigned to accommodate their B&B. Three guest rooms, each with private bath, a large guest deck, and a well-stocked hot beverage nook, were created. The Edgewater Room is the prime choice, featuring ocean view, combination en suite, and private entrance. The Rockcliff Room also has a private entrance and en suite with shower. The Hillcrest Room offers either a king or twins, whichever guests prefer, with private bathroom across the hall. The West Coast design with lots of windows makes the most of the views and pleasant surroundings. Guests will appreciate art collected from many continents, tastefully displayed in the guest sitting room.

Guest Comments: *I wouldn't change a thing, except to stay longer. Thank you for creating such a place of beauty and tranquillity. Your attention to detail is superb.*

Summerhill Menu

Early morning tea and coffee served with a date-nut loaf
Freshly squeezed orange juice
Selection of warm croissants, breads, and freshly baked muffins or scones
Fruit starter
Entreé—a fluffy baked eggroll filled with Parmesan reggiano, black olives, chives, red peppers, mushrooms, and sour cream drizzled with a light cheese dill sauce.

Unicorn Stables

Hosts: Derek & Andrea Sowden
2234 North End Road, SSI V8K 1A7
Phone: (250) 537-9866
Fax: (250) 537-9868
Units: 1 **Rates:** $90

FEATURE: LOCATED ON A PASTORAL ACREAGE, REMINISCENT OF A SOUTHERN HORSE FARM. THE PROPERTY IS WELL MAINTAINED AND THE GROUNDS ARE IMMACULATE. OPENED 1996.

The Carriage Room, a separate building from the house, provides private, comfortable accommodation in a secluded garden setting. Children old enough to manage the ladder to the loft are welcome. The loft provides a great hideaway as well as a cozy sleeping spot with its twin beds, shelves of books, and reading lights. Two skylights make stargazing inevitable. The main floor features a queen bed, sitting area, shower/bath, and kitchenette with microwave. An outside barbeque is also available. The equestrian theme and tasteful country décor make this a delightful place to hide out, relax, and unwind.

Note: Although called Unicorn Stables, the only horse on the property is Andrea's and is not available for riding. This is not a working farm.

Guest Comments: *Enjoyed the setting, peace, and quiet. We are leaving with wonderful memories.*

Mushroom and Onion Egg Bake

A recipe for cheese lovers

1 tbsp vegetable oil	4 green onions, chopped
4 ounces mushrooms, sliced	1 cup low-fat cottage cheese
1 cup sour cream or yogurt	6 eggs
2 tbsp all-purpose flour	1/4 tsp salt
1/8 tsp freshly ground pepper	

Preheat oven to 350 degrees. Grease shallow 1 quart baking dish. Heat oil in medium skillet over medium heat. Add onions and mushrooms and cook until tender. Set aside. In blender or food processor, process cottage cheese until smooth. Add sour cream or yogurt, eggs, flour, salt, pepper, and hot sauce. Process until combined. Stir in onions and mushrooms. Pour into greased dish. Bake about 40 minutes or until knife inserted near centre comes out clean. Makes about 6 servings.

WATER'S EDGE

Host: Helen Tara
327 Price Road, SSI V8K 2E9
Phone: (250) 537-5807
Fax: (250) 537-2862
Units: 2 **Rates:** $110 - $135

Bed & Breakfast
Water's Edge

FEATURE: LOCATED ON THE SHORELINE OF GANGES HARBOUR WITH DIRECT
BEACH ACCESS. OPENED **1989**.

The beautiful gardens bordering the driveway and entrance to Water's Edge are a good indication of what guests can expect from their stay at this oceanside retreat. The design is very accommodating to travellers' needs. A waterfront guest lounge with private entrance, woodstove, and galley includes a great library. One C-View, a spacious en suite room, has a queen and daybed. Sweet Too has an adjoining small bedroom that will comfortably accommodate a third person. Each room has a queen bed. Both are waterview units.

Ganges Harbour lies at your doorstep with its cluster of small islands gracing the scene. Do take time to borrow the rowboat and scout the shoreline—lots of herons, eagles, and sea life.

Guest Comments: *Please adopt me! Even though I am 45 years old!! We've never known such peace! We are going to take a piece of Heaven home with us. We don't want to leave. West Yorkshire, England.*

Homemade Muesli

I have no set amounts for these ingredients. This usually makes a large amount of cereal that I store in large glass jars in the freezer to keep it fresh.
1/4 cup or more margarine or butter
1/4 to 1/2 cup medium brown sugar or honey
1/4 to 1/2 tsp salt

old-fashioned rolled oats	triticale
rye or wheat flakes	sesame seeds
sunflower seeds	poppy seeds
regular rolled oats	coconut
flax seed	whole almonds

Melt margarine or butter in a large frying pan. Add sugar or honey and salt, then the remainder of the ingredients.
Toast on a cookie sheet in the oven at low to medium heat. Turn until lightly toasted throughout. As you remove from oven, add raisins or other dried fruit.

WESTON LAKE INN

Hosts: Susan Evans & Ted Harrison
813 Beaver Point Road, SSI V8K 1X9
Phone: (250) 653-4311
Fax: (250) 653-4340
Units: 3 **Rates:** $95 - $120

FEATURE: WELL-ESTABLISHED B&B ON A HOBBY FARM OVERLOOKING WESTON LAKE. HOSTS ORGANICALLY PRODUCE MANY OF THE INGREDIENTS FOR THEIR SUPERB BREAKFASTS. OPENED 1986.

One of the longest operating B&Bs on Salt Spring, Weston Lake Inn's reputation has been built upon Susan and Ted's dedication.

Appreciating the natural beauty of the place, Susan has enhanced it by creating gorgeous gardens and decorating the house with impeccable taste. She loves sharing her special creation with guests. The two fireside guest lounges are exquisite, one offering a quiet, cozy reading atmosphere and the other being well stocked with movies and games.

Each guest room offers an en suite bath, down duvets, and a theme décor reflecting the name of the room. Original artwork and petit-point (hand done by Ted) adorn the walls. The Heritage Room has a queen and a twin bed. The outdoor hot tub perched above the lake looks out onto a picturesque scene.

Guest Comments: *A beautiful setting, so wonderfully Gulf Island, with a quiet elegance inside. We shall return.*

Weston Lake Inn Menu

Fresh fruit juice
Garden raspberries with crème fraiche
Three cheese scones with garden jams
Homemade granola
Our own eggs scrambled with garden herbs, served with bagels, cream cheese, and lox, topped with optional capers and chopped onion.
Beverage of choice.

WISTERIA GUEST HOUSE

Hosts: Dee Hellicar & Jean Brown
            268 Park Drive, SSI V8K 2S1
Phone: (250) 537-5899
Units: 6 plus cottage   **Rates:** $65

FEATURE: LOCATED IN GANGES ON AN ACRE OF BEAUTIFUL GARDENS. OPENED
1991.

Dee and Jean, locally known as the Wisteria Sisters, are reason enough
to visit Wisteria Guest House. Their high spirits and generous hospitality
are hard to surpass. The main house has six guest rooms, a guest kitchen,
and spacious lounge, all in a separate wing. Bathrooms are shared
between two rooms, and the size of beds varies by room. A self-contained
cottage is also available. All the accommodation is pleasantly decorated
and well maintained.

The guest house is ideal for wedding parties, seminars, reunions,
or bicycle touring groups. Within walking distance of the numerous shops,
galleries, and restaurants of Ganges, Wisteria's convenient location is one of
its main attractions.

In Jean's words, "We take care of the old ones and mother the
young ones."

Guest Comments:

Two sisters of Salt Spring we hear
Are innkeepers without peer
Their rooms are spacious
Their manners so gracious
We're all coming back here next year.

Hollandaise Sauce

(for salmon recipe on page 157)

3 egg yolks	1/4 tsp salt
pinch of pepper	1 tbsp lemon juice
1 tbsp water	4 ounces butter

Place egg yolks, seasonings, and liquid in blender. Melt butter in
saucepan until foaming hot. Blend egg mixture at top speed for 2
seconds. Uncover blender and add hot butter in a slow stream of
droplets (leave out the milk solids at the bottom of the saucepan).

SALT SPRING'S WATERSIDE RESORTS

THE TERM "RESORT" ON SALT SPRING ISLAND refers to commercially zoned waterfront properties with four to twelve cottages on site. Most are family oriented with playgrounds, rowboats or canoes, and beach access.

A request made to one of our local resorts by a guest not wanting to be above the thirteenth floor was deemed rather humorous by Salt Spring standards. A two-storey building is a high-rise to us!

Cottages range in size from studios to three bedroom, but all have indoor bathrooms and some kitchen facilities. Bed sizes vary and many include living room sofabeds to accommodate additional people. Reservations are recommended during the peak season and some places require weekly rentals during July and August. Inquire directly for specifics and current rates.

While quaint and mildly rustic, all facilities are clean, comfortable, and have met B.C. Tourism standards.

This expanse of lawn at Cottage Resort beside calm St. Mary Lake offers a tranquil place to spend a summer afternoon.

COTTAGE RESORT

Host: Pearl Gray
175 Suffolk Road, SSI V8K 1L8
Phone: (250) 537-2214
Fax: (250) 537-2214
Units: 8 cottages, from studio to 3-bedroom **Rates:** $85 - $165

FEATURE: LOCATED ON THE EAST SHORE OF ST. MARY LAKE, FACING SOUTHWEST. GREAT SUNSETS! COTTAGE RENTALS SINCE 1932.

Pearl has been welcoming guests to Cottage Resort since 1991. Eight cottages are situated on 5 1/2 acres of parklike grounds with large picturesque gardens. Decorative touches give each cottage its own comfortable charm. All have furnished decks and some have fireplaces. Cottage #7 houses a jacuzzi tub and fireplace. This is an all-season resort. Unlimited firewood makes it a great cold-weather getaway for couples.

Complimentary canoe and rowboats, a beachside barbeque, play area, and sandy beach provide activities for the whole family.

GREEN ACRES RESORT

Hosts: The Lambert Family
241 Langs Road, SSI V8K 1N3
Phone: (250) 537-2585
Fax: (250) 537-9901
Units: 12 cottages, 1 or 2 bedrooms **Rates:** $95 - $120

FEATURE: LOCATED ON 7 ACRES OF SOUTH-FACING PROPERTY AT THE NORTH END OF ST. MARY LAKE.

Built on a gently sloping bank, each cottage enjoys a serene view of the lake. A stroll through the woods, a paddle boat jaunt on the lake, or swimming from the sandy beach are activities to be enjoyed. Mike Lambert and son Scott have refurbished the cottages to feature woodburning stoves, large private decks with propane barbeques, and fully equipped kitchens. The Homestead Log Cottage is especially charming.

Maple Ridge Cottages

Host: Lauren Sipone
301 Tripp Road, SSI V8K 1K6
Phone: (250) 537-5977
Fax: (250) 537-5977
Units: 3 1-bedroom, 1 2-bedroom   **Rates:** $92 for 2, $132 for 4

Maple Ridge Cottages

FEATURE: LOCATED ON A SECLUDED PART OF ST. MARY LAKE.

At the water's edge there are two docks with canoes, rowboats, windsurfers, and a sailboat for guests' use. Lauren, an accomplished sailor, will often assist novices. Of course both swimming and fishing are also popular activities.

The cedar structures are fully equipped housekeeping cottages. Private sundecks, comfortable furnishings, local artwork, and woodstoves provide a cozy atmosphere.

Spindrift Resort

Hosts: Sharon McCollough & Maureen Bendick
255 Welbury Drive, SSI V8K 2L7
Phone: (250) 537-5311
Units: 6   **Rates:** $95 - $185

spindrift

FEATURE: ON A SIX-ACRE PENINSULA WHERE PATHS WIND UP FROM TWO WHITE-SAND BEACHES THROUGH ARBUTUS AND FIR GROVES.

Maureen and Sharon personally built the six cottages in the 1970s, each with an oceanfront location with all cottages directly overlooking the sea. Each is individually appointed, featuring pottery and paintings by local artists. All cabins have fireplaces and electric heat. Spindrift is a wildlife lover's paradise with eagles, seals, and otters frequently visiting the peninsula to join the herd of deer and resident rabbits who live on the point year round. Small boats are easily launched from the sandy beaches and clamming is excellent. Quiet leashed pets are welcome by prior arrangement. Adult oriented.

HASTINGS HOUSE

Hosts: Mark Gottaas & Judith Hart
160 Upper Ganges Road, SSI V8K 2S2
Phone: (250) 537-2362 or 1-800-661-9255
Fax: (250) 537-5333
E-mail: hasthouse@saltspring.com
Units: 10   **Rates:** $365 - $495

FEATURE: AN EXQUISITE THIRTY-ACRE SEASIDE ESTATE OVERLOOKING GANGES HARBOUR. MEMBER OF CHATEAU-RELAIS.

This world-renowned destination resort consists of guest suites in four tastefully restored buildings. Each room's charming décor is enhanced by eiderdown comforters, oversized bath towels, and stacks of split firewood, wet bars, and specialty touches.

Farm House East & West, Post, and Greenhouse have all been newly renovated this year and now have soaker tubs in each bathroom. Post, a two-room garden cottage set under a large pear tree, features French doors opening out to an ocean view.

All units are quaintly appointed with antiques, wicker or pine furniture, artwork, and distinct fabrics to enhance their theme décor.

Included with accommodation are wake-up hampers delivered to guest suites each morning, full breakfast in the dining room or continental breakfast delivered to guest suites, and afternoon tea in the Manor House.

Dining: Gourmet dining is available in the dining room (jackets required) with a multi-course set menu which changes daily. The most popular choice is the table for two in the kitchen, allowing guests to observe Chef Marcel Kauer preparing each specialty delight.

The Snug also provides set-menu dinners with some lighter options. Neat casual dress is acceptable. Reservations must be made by 1 p.m. for dinner the same evening.

Note: Salt Spring also has hotel/motel accommodations with a total of 80 rooms.

HOSTELS

Salt Spring Island Hostel

Hosts: Mike Ablitt & Paula Davies
640 Cusheon Lake Road
SSI V8K 2C2

Phone: (250)537-4149

HOSTELLING INTERNATIONAL

Units: 2 private rooms, 8-bed male dormitory, 6-bed female dormitory, the Tree House, and 3 teepees. Space for tent camping is also available.

Rates: Private units- $45; Dorms: Members of Hostelling International $14, non-members $18

FEATURE: LOCATED ON TEN PEACEFUL, FORESTED ACRES JUST A SHORT WALK FROM CUSHEON LAKE, THIS RURAL, NATURAL SETTING OFFERS A SAFE, HOME-BASED HOSTEL FOR TRAVELLERS.

Mike Ablitt, the owner of the property, has dedicated the past five years to building this place into a haven for world travellers. And a haven it is!

Paula first visited Salt Spring Island in 1994 while hostelling in B.C. So convinced was she about making the island her home that she asked Mike if she could manage the hostel. Following a short return trip to Toronto to pack up her life, she moved to Salt Spring and still can't say enough about its virtues. Her dynamic personality and overwhelming enthusiasm for her job would inspire anyone in the hospitality business. A short visit with Paula and Mike makes it easy to understand why hostellers from all over the world seek out this destination. Word of mouth has served them well.

Hostelling International is well known for providing safe, clean, affordable accommodation for the adventurous traveller. On Salt Spring Island, a large percentage of guests are single women looking for a safe refuge and a homey atmosphere. The communal lounge and kitchen are comfortably equipped and provide a warm, relaxed atmosphere for striking up new friendships and renewing old ones. Although a social atmosphere prevails with a nightly campfire under the stars, it is not a party house and noise levels and conduct are monitored.

Mike is especially proud of the Tree House he built; it has proved to be the most popular accommodation for visitors as well. Twenty feet off the ground, built around the trunk of a huge cedar tree, the house has a double bed, wicker furniture, and a woodstove. Three teepees are nestled in the outlying wooded areas and are eighteen feet high with an eighteen foot diameter, each providing sleeping space for up to six people.

The maximum stay at a Hostelling International facility is usually three days, but at the Salt Spring Hostel longer stays are often requested and approved. About half the hostel guests are Canadian. Large numbers of hostellers also come from Australia, New Zealand, the Netherlands, Switzerland, Germany, and Britain. People of all cultures and ages, including families with young children, have chosen hostelling as their way of travel, and after meeting Mike and Paula it is easy to understand why!

SIMPLY THE BEST

Room with a View
(not waterfront
property)

Captain's Passage—Welbury Bay Room
Cranberry Ridge—Twig Room
The Partridge House—Studio Suite

Oceanmania
(waterfront with beach
access & views)

Anchorage Cove
Annie's Oceanfront Hideaway
The Beach House—Fulford
Water's Edge

Family Ties
(children welcome)

The Beach House—Sunrise Suite
Blackberry
Cottage Resort
Demery's Retreat
The Partridge House

Dog Gone Pets
(not very many places
accept pets)

The Beach House—Sunrise Suite
Cranberry Ridge
Spindrift Resort

Country Charm
(heritage or
country setting)

The Salt Spring Way
Unicorn Stables
Weston Lake Inn
Beddis House

**Best Places for
Romance**

Annie's Oceanfront Hideaway
 —Garry Oak Room
The Beach House—Starfish Room
Beddis House—Rose Bower Room
Cranberry Ridge—Twig Room
Kitchener House—Kitchener Cottage

Lakeside Fun
(children welcome)

Cottage Resort
Green Acres Resort
Log House
Maple Ridge Cottages

Love That Kitchen

Amblecote
Summerhill Guest House
Weston Lake Inn

Budget Conscious

Becton Croft
The Partridge House
Salt Spring Way
Wisteria Guest House

SALT SPRING BOOKS

SALT SPRING HAS LONG BEEN BLESSED WITH CITIZENS and visitors interested in its history. As a result, a number of fascinating, entertaining accounts of early island life are available to history lovers. Most of the historic summary provided in this book drew on the efforts of writers of the following books. Some of the listed pamphlets are only available on the island itself, while other books from trade publishers are available at general bookstores.

Hamilton, Bea. *Salt Spring Island*. Vancouver: Mitchell Press, 1969.

Hill, Beth et al. *Times Past*. Ganges: Community Arts Council, 1983.

Kahn, Charles. *Hiking the Gulf Islands*. Victoria: Orca Books, 1995.

Killian, Crawford. *Go Do Some Great Thing*. Vancouver: Douglas & McIntyre, 1978.

Koppel, Tom. *Kanaka*. North Vancouver, BC: Whitecap Books, 1995.

Lederman, Jeff. *Cries of the Wild*. Surrey, BC: Heritage House, 1997.

Murray, Peter. *Homesteads and Snug Harbours*. Victoria: Horsdal & Schubart, 1991.

Obee, Bruce. *The Gulf Islands Explorer*. North Vancouver, BC: Whitecap Books, 1990.

Payne, David. *Island Cycling*. Victoria: Orca Books, 1996.

Roberts, Eric. *Salt Spring Sagas*. Ganges, BC: Driftwood, 1962.

Snowden, Mary Ann. *Island Paddling*. Victoria: Orca Books, 1997.

Sweet, Arthur F. *Islands in Trust*. Lantzville, BC: Oolichan Books, 1988.

Toynbee, Richard Mouat. *Snapshots of Early Salt Spring*. Ganges, BC: Mouat's Trading, 1978.

Wilson, Rev. E.F. *Salt Spring Island, British Columbia, 1895*. Ganges, BC: Wilson, 1895.

Yorath, C. J., and H. W. Nasmith. *The Geology of Southern Vancouver Island*. Victoria: Orca Books, 1995.

ELLIE THORBURN

Ellie with her pal, High Jump.

Ellie Thorburn is a former educator with an arts degree in sociology from the University of Windsor. Her interest in arts and gardening is reflected on her property. She enjoys meeting new people and remains involved in many community projects.

On my first visit to Salt Spring in the summer of 1986, it seemed like something out of a novel. The people I met were so tied to their roots, and family history was an inherent part of their everyday lives. While Salt Spring had its own magical splendour and was a great place to visit, I was too much of a city lover to ever think I'd live here. How little I knew! By 1989, for assorted reasons, I left Vancouver behind. Seeking a new home with clean air and natural appeal, I opted for Salt Spring.

In 1990 I opened The Beach House B&B, giving me a new venue to indulge my creative spirit. Soon I was involved as chairperson of the Accommodation Group, director of the Chamber of Commerce, and a member of the Advisory Planning Commission to the Islands Trust. In 1993 I was elected as a director for Tourism Association Vancouver Island (TAVI).

In 1995 I decided to do a major addition to expand my home into a full-fledged bed-and-breakfast. One day during construction, as mud flowed freely, an engineer suggested that I remove precious belongings in case the house slid into the harbour. The house and I survived, wonderful people now enjoy both the new rooms and the upper suite with its enlarged deck. Guests have been complimentary and encouraging. I still enjoy a visit to the city, but this past decade has made me a part of Salt Spring and Salt Spring a part of me.

PEARL GRAY

Pearl Gray came to B.C. from Edmonton in 1976. In Vancouver, this mother of two was both homemaker and businesswoman. She recently completed her B.A. in Art History at the University of British Columbia and has been active in Salt Spring community work with the Chamber of Commerce and Artspring.

When I moved to Salt Spring in May of 1991, I had never lived in a place with less than 300,000 people. Salt Spring had 8000. I soon learned that in a small community, everyone knew everything that you were doing. I had lost the anonymity of the city. But with loss there was gain. To my pleasant surprise, I felt part of a community where people cared about you. In the seven years I have been here, this unique place has allowed me to weave life as a tapestry, the changing seasons ever promoting a range of interests.

As proprietor of Cottage Resort I often work seven days a week attending to guest needs. This is not as arduous as it sounds as my flexible schedule give me time to read extensively and I have discovered the joys of belonging to a book club, sharing literary impressions with a group of other people. In my studio I paint, quilt, and otherwise create. In springtime, Cottage Resort is a plethora of flower gardens, a living palette of colour that I get to play and create in. My business provides constant opportunity to meet my varied guests and industry colleagues. Two years ago I headed a major fund-raising drive to complete the Artspring Building. During winter I like to travel and have visited most continents. Travel writing has become an offshoot of this.

So to my friends in Vancouver who so lovingly wondered if I would be lonely moving to such a small, seemingly isolated place...It's not a bad life.

The Authors' Thoughts

THE EDITOR LET US TURN OUR AUTHOR page into pages because after all the interviews, research, fact verifying, and writing of this manuscript, we wanted to say a few things about Salt Spring on our own. The process of researching this book has prompted our own introspection. With almost twenty years of island time between us, we had to admit seductive Salt Spring has become our "place to be."

In future years we hope to update and expand our book. We see it as an ongoing celebration of the island's past, present, and future. We would like to hear from you with any comments.

As we have come to know more about our island, one fact stands out. Salt Spring is more about "living" than "earning." Most residents have a sincere wish to protect lifestyle and downplay commercialism. In many ways Salt Spring's legacy is that it allows people to be what they choose, to place human experience above the endless economic demands of materialism.

We think that theme has repeated itself throughout this book in interviews with people like Robert Bateman, David Wood, Bev Byron, Bob Andrew, and many others. The process of preparing this book has opened our eyes even further to the sense of community that exists here. We seem to spat like family members who can be very stubborn on home-grown issues. However, when we are criticized from outside or assaulted by some grand new development scheme, we band together to deflect the affront. We rally behind our Islands Trust and keep the outside world in its place.

We have now come to enjoy "country living" and appreciate all the wonderful gifts of a Salt Spring lifestyle. This is our place to be.

PHOTO CREDITS

Akerman, Bob: 8(b), 15(b), 26, 27, 28, 30
Anchorage Cove, 171
Andrew, Marion: 53, 137
Annie's Oceanfront Hideaway, 170
BC Archives: 22 (A-01092) 24(u) (B-06722), 24(m) (H-03525), 24 (1-no ref.),
    32(u) (C-03841), 32(b) (I-26708), 33 (I-26713)
Beddis House, 170
Campbell, Jill Louise: 90
Captain's Passage, 170
Cranberry Ridge, 171
Dayspring Studio: 97
Gray, Pearl: 78, 82, 85, 89, 92, 95, 102, 108, 109, 111, 116, 122, 125, 148, 178
Gulf Island Driftwood: 44, 50, 57, 60, 61, 62, 63, 65, 130, 131, 144(b)
Hagen, Ute: 98
Island Wildlife Natural Care Centre: 105
Karpinski, Ellen: 128 (b)
Kitchener House, 170
Layard, Olive: 167
Litton, Karey: 16
Log House B&B, 171
Onley, Toni: 110
Partridge, Lynne: 129 (u)
Salt Spring Island Hostel, 183
Stevenson, Anne: 35, 36, 42, 55, 66, 72, 128(ur), 138, 144 (m), 151, 156
Summerhill Guest House, 171
Tara, Helen: 128 (mr), 129 (ml, mr, b)
Thorburn, Ellie: 12, 25 (b),67, 74, 76, 126, 127, 141, 142, 170
Toynbee, Richard Mouat: 8 (ul, ml), 11, 13 (u, b), 15 (u, m), 21, 23, 25 (u), 32 (m)
Water's Edge B&B, 171
Weeden, Judy: 119

(u -upper, ur - upper right, ul - upper left, m - middle, ml - middle left, mr - middle
right, b - bottom, bl - bottom left, br - bottom right)

Index